# Sir Fulke Greville's Life of Sir Philip Sidney

## Anonymous

Copyright © BiblioLife, LLC

This book represents a historical reproduction of a work originally published before 1923 that is part of a unique project which provides opportunities for readers, educators and researchers by bringing hard-to-find original publications back into print at reasonable prices. Because this and other works are culturally important, we have made them available as part of our commitment to protecting, preserving and promoting the world's literature. These books are in the "public domain" and were digitized and made available in cooperation with libraries, archives, and open source initiatives around the world dedicated to this important mission.

We believe that when we undertake the difficult task of re-creating these works as attractive, readable and affordable books, we further the goal of sharing these works with a global audience, and preserving a vanishing wealth of human knowledge.

Many historical books were originally published in small fonts, which can make them very difficult to read. Accordingly, in order to improve the reading experience of these books, we have created "enlarged print" versions of our books. Because of font size variation in the original books, some of these may not technically qualify as "large print" books, as that term is generally defined; however, we believe these versions provide an overall improved reading experience for many.

*Sir Fulke Greville's*
# Life of Sir Philip Sidney
etc.

*First Published*
1652

With an Introduction by
Nowell Smith

Late Fellow of New College

*At the Clarendon Press*
MCMVII

Oxford
Printed at the Clarendon Press
By Horace Hart, M.A.
Printer to the University

# INTRODUCTION

Sir Philip Sidney is so familiar and so attractive a name, and Fulke Greville, Lord Brooke, so little known outside the libraries of scholars, that the book which is here republished requires a word or two of introduction for the reader who is not already versed in the subject. It was first published in 1652, twenty-four years after its author's death; and the title, 'The Life of the renowned Sir Philip Sidney' (with other matters; see the title-page), was given to it presumably by the unknown P. B., the editor, certainly not by Greville himself. In a manuscript copy of the work, of which we shall hear more hereafter, the title is simply 'A Dedication'; and Greville's primary object was to dedicate his poems, 'these exercises of my youth,' as he calls them, 'to that Worthy Sir Philip Sidney, so long since departed.' The Dedication spreads out, in the unchannelled abundance of our earlier prose and the retired soliloquizing of Greville's older age, into a 'Treatise', in which the primary object is clean forgotten in the rush of the writer's memory of those two subjects

of

of so much greater importance, his friend, Sir Philip, and his mistress, Queen Elizabeth. The treatise is indeed our first authority for some of the well-known stories of Sidney, notably that of the cup of water at Zutphen, and that of the quarrel with the Earl of Oxford in the tennis court (Greville, however, does not give the earl's name); but it is at once much less and much more than a regular biography of Sidney. There are no dates, no details of personal appearance, place of abode, habits, friends and acquaintances; nothing of marriage; scarcely anything of life at court; nothing even of Sidney's literary pursuits, except an interesting criticism of the *Arcadia* solely from the point of view of the political philosopher.

Here, in fact, we have the matter in a nutshell. In all that he writes, except the love poems of the series named *Caelica*, Greville writes as a political philosopher and moralist. Even in *Caelica* the thinker dominates the lover, and often banishes the artist: the rest of the poems, including the plays, are, even avowedly (cp. *Life of Sidney*, chs. 14 and 18), political philosophy in verse. The bulk of them are called 'Treatises'—'a Treatise of Religion'; 'a Treatie of Humane Learning'; 'an Inquisition upon Fame and Honour'; 'a Treatise of Monarchy',

## Introduction

archy', which is divided into 'sections' with such titles as 'Of weak-minded Tyrants', 'Cautions against these weak extremities,' 'Of Lawes,' 'Of Commerce.' These treatises 'were first intended', Greville writes (*Sidney*, ch. 14), 'to be for every act [in the Tragedies] a chorus': but 'with humble sayles after I had once ventured upon this spreading *Ocean* of Images, my apprehensive youth [i.e. youth which naturally grasps at whatever it sees], for lack of a well touched compasse, did easily wander beyond proportion'. The tragedies themselves were political, especially the one which Greville destroyed, *Antonie and Cleopatra*, 'many members in that creature (by the opinion of those few eyes which saw it) having some childish wantonnesse in them, apt enough to be construed or strained to a personating of vices in the present Governors and government.' The object in all three of them was 'to trace out the high waies of ambitious Governours, and to shew in the practice, that the more audacity, advantage, and good successe such Soveraignties have, the more they hasten to their owne desolation and ruine' (ch. 18). Similarly very much the greater part of the *Life of Sidney* consists of reflections upon the political problems of Elizabeth's reign, upon Sidney's views on this subject, upon Elizabeth's beth's methods of government. Greville, like Sidney and Drake and most of the 'stirring Spirits' (ch. 8) of that time, was strongly anti-Spanish and anti-Papal. His denunciations of Spanish ambition and Papal subservience are so persistent that only the abundance and the quaintness of his language save them from becoming monotonous. There can be little doubt that part of the scorn and displeasure, with which in his later years he alludes, in terms however general, to the degeneracy of the times, was due to his memory of the days of his early manhood, when the struggle with Spain worked together with the commercial enterprise, fostered by the discovery of the New World and the intellectual awakening of the Renaissance, to give a zest to political life, which was more and more lacking in the reign of James I, and even in the last years of Elizabeth herself. Not that Greville was ever, in all probability, a very light-hearted optimist or an adventurous man of action. One pictures him as usually throwing his influence on the side of prudence in his relations with his two more brilliant friends and kinsmen, Sidney [1] and, afterwards, the rash and unfortunate

[1] Cp. p. 74, where Greville relates how he inspired 'that ingenuous spirit of Sir Philip's' with suspicion of Drake's whole-heartedness in their projected enterprise.

Essex.

Essex. His own career, too, was that of a man who was more apt to fill useful and more or less lucrative employments and to steer clear of the extremes of partisanship than to put his fortune to the touch in any daring scheme of ambition. He had his strong sympathies, and they were not with the Cecils[1]; but he had no open breach with them, and he filled various posts while they still lived, though he evidently blossomed out again in his old age after the Earl of Salisbury's death in 1612. The following pages will show that he was genuinely devoted to Queen Elizabeth; and it is clear that she regarded him with favour as a courtier who could be trusted. He started his political career with offices in the principality of Wales, of which his friend's father, Sir Henry Sidney, was Lord President. He received various grants of land and emoluments, was knighted in 1597, and made Treasurer of Marine Causes in 1599–1600. Bacon records that 'Sir Fulke Grevill had much and private access to Queen Elizabeth, which he used honourably, and did many men good: yet he would say merrily of himself "That he was like Robin Goodfellow: for when the maids spilt the milk-pans or

[1] Cp. pp. 217 foll., and the story of the fall of Essex, pp. 156 foll.

kept

kept any racket, they would lay it upon Robin: so what tales the ladies about the Queen told her, or other bad offices that they did, they would put it upon him"'. Whatever they said about him, he was, as another writer tells us, 'a constant courtier of the ladies'; and the fact that he never married no doubt contributed to his having 'the longest lease and the smoothest time, without rub, of any of her [Elizabeth's] favourites'.[1] In the second year of James I he was granted Warwick Castle, then a ruin, which he made into the splendid pile which it still remains. Internal evidence and the probabilities of the case point to the time between the death of Henry IV of France[2] in 1610 and that of the Earl of Salisbury in 1612,[3] as that in which the so-called *Life of Sidney* was composed. Soon after the later of these two dates Greville was made Under-Treasurer,

[1] Sir Robert Naunton, *Fragmenta Regalia* (1642), p. 30: quoted, with the passage from Bacon (Spedding, vii, p. 158), by Grosart, *Lord Brooke's Works*, vol. i, p. lxx.
[2] Cp. p. 31.
[3] From the manner in which Salisbury is spoken of on pp. 217–9, combined with the absence of any allusion to his death, I think it probable that he was still alive when the treatise was written. The fact that Greville's tragedy *Mustapha* was, perhaps piratically, published in 1609, may have some significance in connexion with the date of the *Dedication* of his poems to the memory of Sidney.

and

and then Chancellor of the Exchequer (1614), a Privy Councillor, and a Gentleman of the Bedchamber. In 1620 he was created Lord Brooke of Beauchamps-Court; and the Calendars of State Papers show that in spite of his advanced age—'Age and sickness, the gentlemen ushers of death,' as he writes with regard to himself in 1625[1]—he was an active member of the House of Lords and of the administration. A long letter which he wrote to the Duke of Buckingham in 1623, reads like a piece of the *Life of Sidney*: the ambition and intrigues of Spain and the Papacy are denounced in the same picturesque language. Lord Brooke lived on into the reign of Charles I. On Sept. 1, 1628, he was stabbed in the back by a body-servant, Mr. Ralph Haywood, who was apparently enraged by being unmentioned in his master's will, and who 'to consummate the Tragedy, went into another roome, and having lock't the dore, pierced his own bowells with a sword'.[2] A contemporary lampoon gives the

---

[1] Grosart, vol. iv, p. 320.
[2] Dugdale's *Warwickshire*, pp. 571–3; much the same account of Greville is given by Dugdale in his *Baronage*, vol. ii, pp. 442–3. These passages form the main source of information about Greville's career. The facts are given more fully and with much comment of doubtful value in Dr. Grosart's Memorial-Introduction, *Lord Brooke's Works*, vol i.

dead

kept any racket, they would lay it upon Robin: so what tales the ladies about the Queen told her, or other bad offices that they did, they would put it upon him"'. Whatever they said about him, he was, as another writer tells us, 'a constant courtier of the ladies'; and the fact that he never married no doubt contributed to his having 'the longest lease and the smoothest time, without rub, of any of her [Elizabeth's] favourites'.[1] In the second year of James I he was granted Warwick Castle, then a ruin, which he made into the splendid pile which it still remains. Internal evidence and the probabilities of the case point to the time between the death of Henry IV of France[2] in 1610 and that of the Earl of Salisbury in 1612,[3] as that in which the so-called *Life of Sidney* was composed. Soon after the later of these two dates Greville was made Under-Treasurer,

[1] Sir Robert Naunton, *Fragmenta Regalia* (1642), p. 30: quoted, with the passage from Bacon (Spedding, vii, p. 158), by Grosart, *Lord Brooke's Works*, vol. i, p. lxx.
[2] Cp. p. 31.
[3] From the manner in which Salisbury is spoken of on pp. 217–9, combined with the absence of any allusion to his death, I think it probable that he was still alive when the treatise was written. The fact that Greville's tragedy *Mustapha* was, perhaps piratically, published in 1609, may have some significance in connexion with the date of the *Dedication* of his poems to the memory of Sidney.

and

## Introduction

and then Chancellor of the Exchequer (1614), a Privy Councillor, and a Gentleman of the Bedchamber. In 1620 he was created Lord Brooke of Beauchamps-Court; and the Calendars of State Papers show that in spite of his advanced age—'Age and sickness, the gentlemen ushers of death,' as he writes with regard to himself in 1625 [1]—he was an active member of the House of Lords and of the administration. A long letter which he wrote to the Duke of Buckingham in 1623, reads like a piece of the *Life of Sidney*: the ambition and intrigues of Spain and the Papacy are denounced in the same picturesque language. Lord Brooke lived on into the reign of Charles I. On Sept. 1, 1628, he was stabbed in the back by a body-servant, Mr. Ralph Haywood, who was apparently enraged by being unmentioned in his master's will, and who 'to consummate the Tragedy, went into another roome, and having lock't the dore, pierced his own bowells with a sword'.[2] A contemporary lampoon gives the

[1] Grosart, vol. iv, p. 320.
[2] Dugdale's *Warwickshire*, pp. 571-3; much the same account of Greville is given by Dugdale in his *Baronage*, vol. ii, pp. 442-3. These passages form the main source of information about Greville's career. The facts are given more fully and with much comment of doubtful value in Dr. Grosart's Memorial-Introduction, *Lord Brooke's Works*, vol i.

dead

dead Lord Brooke a bad character for avarice —a vice which was perhaps never more in vogue than in the days of the Tudors, when the confiscation of religious property and the exploitation of the New World whetted the thirst for gold. And Greville was conspicuously one of the new nobility, which built its fortunes, its Warwick castles and Beauchamps-Courts, out of the ruins of the mediaeval baronage and the mediaeval Church. But whatever were the rights of his difference with his servant, the antiquaries Camden and Speed, and the poet Daniel and others bear witness to his generosity as a patron of letters; and he endowed a chair of History at Cambridge, showing his Puritan tendencies [1] and causing much displeasure to Laud, by appointing the Dutch scholar, Isaac Dorislaus, to be the first professor. He died on Sept. 30, 1628, and was buried in a monument of black and white marble which he had erected in his lifetime, in the Collegiate Church of the Virgin at Warwick, with the inscription: 'Fulke Grevil, Servant to Queene Elizabeth, Councellor to King James, and Frend to S<sup>r</sup> Philip Sydney. Trophaeum Peccati.'

As an historical document the so-called

[1] Greville's strong sympathy with the Reformation is always coming out; for one decisive passage cp. below, pp. 216–7.

*Life*

*Life of Sidney* is of considerable importance; and for that-reason I have spent great pains on supplying, by means of accurate notes of a somewhat dry and forbidding appearance, the materials for arriving as closely as may be at the words which the author actually wrote. This ought to have been unnecessary, as the late Dr. Grosart professed and doubtless intended to do the same. Lovers of literature, who happen to have scholarly instincts and training, can never speak of enthusiastic antiquaries like Dr. Grosart without compunction. On the one hand they admire the generous expenditure of time and money which Dr. Grosart gave to his many 'labours of love'. On the other hand they can only look aghast on the mass of inaccurate statements and worthless judgements which swell the undigested bulk of his editions. The gratitude which they are anxious to feel as they enter into the fruits of his labour is thwarted by the double labour which they have to expend in correcting his mistakes and verifying the rest of his statements. I should have preferred to do the work of correction tacitly, but unfortunately Dr. Grosart had another failing, which is not however confined to the unscholarly amateur of letters. He had a mistaken confidence in his own merits, and an absurd way of expressing it by belittling

belittling those of his predecessors. Thus he speaks of the only other reprint of the *Life of Sidney* besides his own, which was executed by Sir Egerton Brydges at his Lee Priory Press in 1816, as 'exceptionally slovenly and unworthy'. This is the very reverse of the truth.¹ Again, having the opportunity of being the first to publish the *Life* according to a MS. copy of it existing in the Library of Trinity College, Cambridge, he exalts that MS. to a pinnacle of excellence upon the strength of a collation not made by himself,² and pursues the text as hitherto printed with a ceaseless stream of 'P grossly misprints', 'P misreads.' He makes no attempt to weigh the comparative value of M (i.e. the MS. at Trinity College) and P (the printed text of 1652). He seems in a vague way to have regarded M as the source of P, which it certainly was not; but he does not even report the readings of the two texts correctly nor apparently pay the least regard to the sense as a guide to his choice between them where they are in conflict.³ The character of his critical

¹ I speak from an examination of the book: but I also notice with satisfaction that Mr. Sidney Lee in his account of Greville in the *Dict. Nat. Biog.* speaks of Sir Egerton Brydges' reprint being done 'with much care'.
² The collation was made by Mr. W. Aldis Wright: Grosart, vol. i, p. xii; vol. iv, p. vii.
³ Perhaps the most glaring of Grosart's editorial

work

## Introduction

work will be sufficiently evident from the notes at the end of this volume. I have felt bound to be outspoken on the subject; but I have spoken with reluctance, and I should like to end by saying that, with all its faults, Grosart's edition of Lord Brooke's Works has the great merit of bringing together a body of writings both in prose and verse which well deserved to be revived for lovers of literature.

The textual criticism of the *Life of Sidney* is a problem, or rather part of a problem,[1] which I have not had time or opportunity thoroughly to attempt to solve. By the hospitality of Dr. Henry Jackson and the kind permission of the authorities of Trinity College I was able to make a collation of M at Cambridge; and I have quoted its readings wherever they seemed to be of the least importance, whether as improving the text or as throwing light upon the divergence between M and P. The differences of reading are very numerous, and vary from minute details to serious discrepancies. The most

faults, if we consider the slavish way in which he follows M in impossible readings, is his omission to record superior readings of his idol; cp. notes on p. 10, l. 9; p. 18, l. 4 from bot.; p. 78, l. 4; p. 83, par. 2, l. 4 from bot.; p. 87, par. 2, l. 1; p. 95, par. 2, l. 9, &c.

[1] MSS. of nearly all Greville's writings exist at Warwick Castle, and were collated by Grosart.

interesting

xvi        *Introduction*

interesting places are naturally those where M contains matter which is absent from P.[1] One of these[2] is especially interesting because it contains a sort of palinode to a somewhat unfavourable account of Sir Francis Drake, and from the words with which it is introduced ('Yet to deale trulie with the dead') would, if there were not abundant evidence to the contrary, tempt one to suppose that the bulk of the *Life* was written before Drake's death in Jan. 1595/6. Only one degree less interesting are the passages omitted by M, but contained in P,[3] since these prove that the omissions of P, just spoken of, are not due to a negligent copying of M or its archetype. Thirdly, among the mass of differences which have only an importance as textual evidence, there are a few curious *variae lectiones*,[4] which seem, together with the omissions and insertions, to prove that M and P represent two different recensions of the text made, in all probability,[5]

[1] See notes on p. 77, end of par. 2; p. 89, ditto; p. 132, ll. 11-13.
[2] p. 77.
[3] See notes on p. 53, l. 12; p. 84, par. 3, l. 7; p. 91, l. 6; p. 97, l. 4 from bot.
[4] See especially notes on p. 106, l. 3 from bot.; p. 108, l. 8; p. 115, l. 5.
[5] Any other supposition is, in the first place, fantastic. In the second place, there exist at Warwick Castle,

by

## Introduction

by the author himself. Both M and P have a good many mistakes which arise from the inattention of the scribe or the compositor, and others due to inability to decipher their originals. Considering the practice of amateurs of literature in those days to circulate their compositions among their friends without having them printed, there is nothing surprising in the fact that M and P must be derived from different versions: and I cannot at present, even if it is not now an insoluble question, determine which version has the better claim to represent the author's *summa manus*.

Nor is the problem one of greater importance than textual problems are apt to be. Any scientific investigation is fascinating to the investigator; and any increase in the accurate knowledge of an author's text is not without its value. But this treatise of Greville's is not one of the rare books in which the restoration of a desperate text is the indispensable preliminary to an intelligent reading of the work. I have attempted, if I may combine metaphors somewhat after Greville's own manner, to kill two birds with

MSS. of Greville's other works, partly in his own handwriting, partly in a scribe's, but with corrections in Greville's, and all of them containing many readings different from the printed texts.

one stone in this edition; but I do not wish to fall between two stools. Though I hope I have done something for the student who may wish to use Greville's treatise as an historical document, my chief desire is that lovers of literature may share the pleasure which it gives me to wander in the 'carelessordered garden' of this old Elizabethan moralist, to be stirred by his meditative eloquence, to fill the ear with his noble rhythms, to please the fancy with his luxuriant images and metaphors, and to find a zest even in tracking his meaning through his devious syntax. For Greville in his prose, as in his verse, is an obscure writer, even for the days before Hobbes and Dryden. The general trend of his argument is clear enough, and the colours of his 'map' of European politics (to use a favourite word of his) have the freshness of the first-hand observer, even though the lines are sometimes drawn with the wavering hand of memory. But in detail he is often very difficult. Now and again this is due to some defect in the transmission of the text. More often the cause is the punctuation, which follows no consistent system and yet is, as a rule, the result of deliberate intention. But the vagaries of Greville's punctuation are really part of the irregular character of his style; and his style means

## Introduction    xix

means his thought, for, though he loves quaint metaphors and similes, he is no mere verbal acrobat, nor is his bewildering syntax a work of affectation.[1] He luxuriates in words, phrases, metaphors, allusions, like all the Elizabethans[2]; one picturesque expression trips over another; an epithet suggests a new turn of thought, and the sentence cannot keep up with the sudden shifting of the course. At the same time he usually retains in his own mind the thread of his argument, and comes back to it, in spite of intervening stops and subjects, with an unconscious abrupt-

---

[1] Motley several times speaks of Greville as a 'euphuist', but this much-abused term is not in any important degree applicable to Greville.

[2] Every one knows that the language of the Elizabethans is surcharged with metaphor; but nowhere, except perhaps in Bacon's Essays, are the metaphors and similes more abundant than in Greville. Many of his images are very vivid. They occur on every page, but a few of the more striking are p. 66, l 7; p. 74, l. 3 from bot.; p. 86, l. 5; p. 94, l. 3; p. 108, l. 5 from bot.; p. 167, l. 5 and 5 from bot.; p. 179, l. 7 from bot.; p. 212, l. 6 from bot.; p. 224, l. 7. Some of the words of which Greville is especially fond are 'selfnesse', 'wind-blown,' 'to wave,' 'rack,' 'map,' 'noun-adjective-natured,' 'undertaker,' and others to which attention is called in the notes on the text. He is also fond of such phrases as 'contented and contenting' (p. 197), 'successive and successful' (p. 209), 'the blessed and blessing presence of this unmatchable Queen and woman' (p. 215).

ness which bewilders the reader unless he holds on to the thread very fast. The same characteristics mark Greville's poetry. It is full of good things—strong phrases, pointed apophthegms, quaint and suggestive metaphors and allusions; but even more than in the prose, certainly with a more deterrent effect upon the reader who expects to find a poem in the first place a work of art, grammar and proportion are constantly forgotten. But although one cannot help seeing in Greville, as in other minds which, though acute and even deep, are yet not of the first order of power, that want of perfect control which soon produces the exaggeration, the paradox, the verbal juggling and fantastic imagery of a decadent style like that of the 'metaphysical' poets, in Greville himself neither failings nor virtues are the stereotyped characteristics of a 'school' or a 'style'. His first interest is in the thoughts which he wants to express; and it is for this reason that his expression, however faulty, has the charm of sincerity, and gives one an idea of originality of mind. The impression is deepened by a somewhat sardonic humour which plays with similarities of sound or contrasts of sense, a sort of punning without elaboration or finish, but suggestive sometimes of contempt, sometimes of a certain restrained passion. Finally, and
for

for the second time, in spite of, and often in the midst of, his oracular obscurity, Greville is often touched by moral and intellectual passion to a fine nobility of utterance, and in these passages he haunts the ear with that solemn and rich and varied rhythm which is the peculiar glory of Elizabethan and Jacobean prose. I know few chapters in any book of a more sustained meditative eloquence than the third of this treatise, and few passages of finer rhythm than the last paragraph of that chapter.

NOWELL SMITH.

WINCHESTER, 1906.

## NOTE

I desire to thank the friends with whom I have discussed difficulties of interpretation, especially Mr. H. J. Hardy, Professor Walter Raleigh, and Mr. H. A. L. Fisher; also the readers of the Clarendon Press for their admirable, though far from unusual, care in correcting my proofs.

# CONTENTS OF THE TREATISE

## CHAP. I.

|  | PAGE |
|---|---|
| Introduction Reason for writing. | 1-4 |
| Parentage and its effects. | 4-6 |
| Boyhood | 6, 7 |
| Travels with Languet. Reflections on their friendship. | 7-11 |
| Sidney's *Arcadia* and reflections on fainéant kings, &c. | 11-16 |
| Further reflections on *Arcadia* Sidney's desire to have it burnt. Not a professional writer. His personal influence and charm. | 16-18 |

## CHAP. II.

Other testimonies to Sidney from the dead (the living being too selfishly jealous): leads on to disquisition on William of Nassau and a conversation Greville had with him in Delft, on Spanish ambition, Austrian diplomacy, &c., 19-26
and finally William on himself, 26
and on Sidney, recommending Sidney to Elizabeth. 27
Sidney objects to Greville telling Elizabeth, and so illustrates his own character. 27-29
Earl of Leicester's testimony, as Governor of Low Countries 29
Sir Francis Walsingham's testimony. 29, 30

## CHAP. III.

| Testimonies of Princes and Governors. | 31, 32 |
|---|---|
| Of Mendoza an enemy. | 32, 33 |
| Of Universities, soldiers, artists, authors, men of affairs, &c. | 33 |
| Value of such a man to the State. | 34, 35 |
| 'The ancient Majestie of noble and true dealing.' | 35 |
| Loyalty to Reformed Religion. | 35, 36 |
| Contrast of Sidney's greatness with *usual* great men. | 37, 38 |

CHAP. IV.

## CHAP. IV.

|  | PAGE |
|---|---|
| Sidney held no high office: but universally respected. | 39, 40 |

His embassy to Emperor Rudolf. he stirs up the German Princes to combine with England against Spain and Rome. 41-45

## CHAP. V.

Sidney's reasons against proposed marriage of Elizabeth with the Duke of Anjou; drawn largely from the marriage of Mary with Philip of Spain. 45-60

## CHAP. VI.

Sidney tenders his advice direct to the Queen. Contrasted with courtiers. He is honest, but holds his own. 60-63
The quarrel of the tennis court (with Earl of Oxford—name not given). 63-69

## CHAP. VII.

Proposed expedition with Drake. Philip Sidney not allowed to go, but given employment under his uncle, the Earl of Leicester, in the Low Countries. 70-78

## CHAP. VIII.

Sidney's survey of the contemporary state of European politics:
| | |
|---|---|
| England. | 79, 80 |
| France. | 81 |
| The States of the Empire and the Hanseatic Cities, their danger from Spain and Rome. | 81-83 |
| Poland, Denmark, Sweden. | 83-85 |
| The Switzers, the Italian States, Muscovy, Turkey. | 85, 86 |
| The power of Spain in Europe and the West Indies. | 86, 87 |
| Insufficiency of a war in the Netherlands. | 87-89 |

## CHAP. IX.

Sidney's suggested measures against Spain, 90-94
and capture of a French town in support of the reformed religion. 94-98
Possible league of England and France and German Princes.
99-101
Savoy

## xxiv  Contents of the Treatise

|  | PAGE |
|---|---|
| Savoy might join, and Venice, | 102–104 |
| and the Italian States. England might occupy the Kingdom of Sicily. | 104, 105 |
| The Pope would probably support or not oppose the allies. | 105, 106 |
| Elizabeth to restore balance of power. | 106, 107 |
| Her previous knowledge of Spanish aims. | 107, 108 |
| Failing this European combination, take up Drake's work of striking at the West Indies. | 109 |

## CHAP. X.

| | |
|---|---|
| Reasons for attacking the Spanish Indies. | 110–113 |
| Spanish oppression of America | 113–116 |
| would ultimately be avenged by God. | 116, 117 |
| Sidney projects an attack on Nombre de Dios or some neighbouring harbour, | 117 |
| and obtains promise of support from the United Provinces and from thirty gentlemen of England. | 118 |
| Motives for the expedition. | 119 |

## CHAP. XI.

| | |
|---|---|
| Sidney goes to the Low Countries as Governor of Flushing and a General of Horse. | 120, 121 |
| The surprise of Axel. | 121 |
| Sir William Brown's attempt on Gravelines | 121–125 |
| Sidney prevents a quarrel between Leicester and Hollock. | 125, 126 |

## CHAP. XII.

| | |
|---|---|
| Sidney's wound at Zutphen and lingering sickness | 127–135 |

## CHAP. XIII.

| | |
|---|---|
| Sidney's last moments. | 135–140 |
| Sidney might perhaps have become Duke of the Netherlands. | 141, 142 |
| Reflections on relations of England and the Netherlands. | 142–144 |
| The States of Zealand request to be allowed to bury Sidney. | 144, 145 |

CHAP. XIV.

## CHAP. XIV.

|  | PAGE |
|---|---|
| How Greville came to write poetry. | 145–150 |
| The Treatises, originally intended as Choruses to the Tragedies. | 150–156 |
| The fate of Essex, Greville's kinsman | 156–161 |

## CHAP. XV.

| Policy of Queen Elizabeth in regard to religion and to continental affairs; | 162–173 |
|---|---|
| in regard to Royal Prerogative and to Favourites ; | 173–183 |

## CHAP. XVI.

| her household ; | 183–185 |
|---|---|
| her rewards; | 185–187 |
| the clergy. | 187 |
| Parliament and the Council. | 187, 188 |
| The nobles, and the yeomanry. | 189, 190 |
| Her caution and moderation in use of monarchy | 190–197 |
| Her success in asking Parliament for money, and her use of it to defend the coasts, | 197, 198 |
| to maintain the navy, support voyages, fisheries, &c. | 198, 199 |
| Her naval officers. | 199–203 |
| Her merchants, and her policy in regard to the Flushingers and Dunkirkers. | 203 |
| Her treatment of the Universities | 203, 204 |
| Summary. | 204, 205 |

## CHAP. XVII.

| Additional instances of Elizabeth's policy in regard to Spain. | 205–215 |
|---|---|
| Reasons for Greville writing this treatise and not a regular history of Queen Elizabeth, and for not publishing in his lifetime. | 215–220 |

## CHAP. XVIII.

| Object, arguments, and style of Greville's Tragedies. | 221–225 |
|---|---|

# THE LIFE
## Of the Renowned
### Sr *PHILIP SIDNEY*.

WITH

The true Intereſt of *England* as it then ſtood in relation to all Forrain Princes: And particularly for ſuppreſſing the power of *Spain* Stated by Him.

His principall Actions, Counſels, Deſignes, and Death.

Together with a ſhort Account of the Maximes and Policies uſed by Queen *Elizabeth* in her Government.

---

Written by Sir FULKE GREVIL Knight, Lord BROOK, a Servant to Queen *Elizabeth*, and his Companion & Friend.

---

*LONDON*,
Printed for *Henry Seile* over againſt St *Dunſtans* Church in Fleet-ſtreet.
MDCLII

Most humbly,
To the Right Honorable
THE
## COUNTESSE
OF
## *SVNDERLAND.*

Since Madam,

*Both your Bloud, and Vertues do so strongly Intitle you to this well-limb'd Piece; it would be a stain upon the Publisher, to enshrine it to any other Name but yours. Who can protect the story*

## The Epistle

*of a* Sidney, *but a* Sidney's Name? *Thus his* Matchless Poem, *seem'd providentially by him impatronag'd unto his* Peerless Sister. *And this (Madam) being another of his* meaner Monuments, *disdains Address to any other Alliance but his own. Here at your feet (by no despicable Pen) the History of our Nations Wonder lies; Whose large spread Fame, your noble Meene improves, and convinces the World of this Truth, That not only the Endowments of Nature, but even the Enoblements of the Mind, and Genius, are many times inherent in the Bloud and Linage. Some Families are privileg'd from Heaven*

## Dedicatory.

*Heaven in Excellencies, which now and then in particular Branches, like new Stars, appear and beautifie the sphere they shine in. And doubtless if the departed into Happiness, have any knowledge of our* humane Vicissitudes, *his gallant Soul looks down with Contentment, to see the Honour of his House continued in your* unblemisht Merit. *Which, taking all, may excuse the presumption that I can be charged with, who not pretending to the Authorage, have thought I could not doe more right, either to* him, *or the* subject *of the discourse, than to inscribe it to* Her, *who like* day in

## The Epistle

*in this* Ecclipse *of* Honour, *enlightning our* Western Orb, *hath ambition'd me to make this offering from,*

Madam,

The meanest of your

most obedient Servants,

*P.B.*

THE

# THE
# Life of the Renowned
## Sr *PHILIP SIDNEY*

### *CHAP. I.*

THe difference which I have found between times, and confequently the changes of life into which their naturall viciffitudes doe violently carry men, as they have made deep furrowes of impreffions into my heart, fo the fame heavy wheeles caufe me to retire my thoughts from free traffique with the world, and rather feek comfortable eafe or imployment in the fafe memory of dead men, than difquiet in a doubtfull converfation amongft the living. Which I ingenuoufly confeffe, to be one chief motive of dedicating thefe exercifes of my youth to that Worthy Sir *Philip Sidney*, fo long fince departed.

departed. For had I grounded my ends upon active Wifedomes of the prefent, or fought Patronage out of hope, or fear in the future; Who knowes not, that there are fome Noble friends of mine, and many Honourable Magiftrates yet living, unto whom both my Fortune, and Reputation were, and are far more fubject? But befides this felf-refpect of Dedication, the debt I acknowledge to that Gentleman is farre greater, as with whom I fhall ever account it honour to have been brought up: and in whom the life it felf of true worth, did (by way of example) far exceed the pictures of it in any moral Precepts. So that (if my creation had been equal) it would have proved as eafie for me, to have followed his patern, in the practice of reall vertue, as to engage my felf into this *Characterifticall* kind of Poefie: in defence whereof he hath written fo much, as I fhall not need to fay any thing. For that this reprefenting of vertues, vices, humours, counfells, and actions of men in feigned, and unfcandalous Images, is an inabling of free-
born

born fpirits to the greateft affaires of States: he himfelf hath left fuch an inftance in the too fhort fcene of his life, as I fear many Ages will not draw a line out of any other mans fphere to parallel with it.

For my own part, I obferved, honoured, and loved him fo much; as with what caution foever I have paffed through my dayes hitherto among the living, yet in him I challenge a kind of freedome even among the dead. So that although with *Socrates*, I profeffe to know nothing for the prefent; yet with *Neſtor* I am delighted in repeating old newes of the ages paft; and will therefore ftir up my drooping memory touching this mans worth, powers, wayes, and defignes: to the end that in the tribute I owe him, our nation may fee a Sea-mark, rais'd upon their native coaft, above the levell of any private Pharos abroad: and fo by a right Meridian line of their own, learn to fayl through the ftraits of true vertue, into a calm, and fpacious Ocean of humane honour.

It is ordinary among men to obferve the races of horfes, and breeds of other cattle. But few confider, that as divers humors mixt in mens bodies make different complexions; fo every Family hath, as it were, divers predominant qualities in it: which, as they are tempered together in Marriage, give a certain tincture to all the defcent. In my time, I have obferved it in many houfes, efpecially in this. Sir *Henry Sidney* his Father was a man of excellent naturall wit, large heart, fweet converfation: and fuch a Governour, as fought not to make an end of the State in himfelf, but to plant his own ends in the profperity of his Countrey. Witnes his found eftablifhments both in *Wales*, and *Ireland*, where his Memory is worthily gratefull unto this day: how unequall, & bitter foever the cenfure of Provincialls is ufually, againft fincere Monarchall Governours, efpecially fuch, as though in worth and place fuperior, are yet in their own degrees of heraldry, inferior to them.

On the other fide, his Mother, as fhe
was

was a woman by defcent of great Nobility, fo was fhe by nature of a large ingenuous fpirit. Whence, as it were even racked with native ftrengths, fhee chofe rather to hide her felf from the curious eyes of a delicate time, than come up on the ftage of the world with any manner of difparagement, the mifchance of ficknefle having caft fuch a kind of veile over her excellent beauty, as the modefty of that fex doth many times upon their native, and heroicall fpirits.

So that it may probably be gathered, that this clearneffe of his Fathers judgement, and ingenious fenfibleneffe of his Mothers, brought forth fo happy a temper in this well-mixt Ofspring of theirs, as (without envy be it fpoken) Sir *Philip* deferves to be accompted amongft thofe eminent Plants of our foyl, which blaft, or bite not, but rather ftatuminate, and refrefh the Vines, Corn, Fruits, or whatfoever groweth under their fhaddows. And as he was their Firft-born, fo was he not the contraction, but the extenfion of their ftrength,
and

and the very acme, and perfect type of it.

Of whose Youth I will report no other wonder, but this; That though I lived with him, and knew him from a child, yet I never knew him other than a man: with such staiednesse of mind, lovely, and familiar gravity, as carried grace, and reverence above greater years. His talk ever of knowledge, and his very play tending to enrich his mind: So as even his teachers found something in him to observe, and learn, above that which they had usually read, or taught. Which eminence, by nature, and industry, made his worthy Father stile Sir *Philip* in my hearing (though I unseen) *Lumen familiæ suæ*. But why doe I mention this relative harmony of worth between Father and Son? Did not his Country soon after take knowledge of him as a Light, or leading Star to every degree within her? Are not the Arts and Languages, which enabled him to Travail at fourteen years old, and in his Travail to win reverence amongst the chief Learned men

men abroad, Witneſſes beyond exception, that there was great inequality of worth and goodneſſe in him ?

Inſtance that reverend *Languet*, mentioned for honours ſake in Sir *Philip's Arcadia*, learned *uſque ad miraculum*; wiſe by the conjunction of practice in the world, with that well-grounded Theory of Books, & much valued at home; till this great Worth (even in a Gentlemans fortune) being diſcovered for a dangerous inſtrument againſt *Rome* and *Spain*, by ſome ſparkles got light enough, rather to ſeek employment elſwhere, than to tarry, and be driven out of his own Country with diſparagement. In *Franckford* he ſettles, is entertained Agent for the Duke of *Saxony*, and an under-hand Miniſter for his own King. Lodged he was in *Wechels* houſe, the Printer of *Franckford*, where Sir *Philip* in travail chancing likewiſe to become a gueſt, this ingenious old mans fulneſſe of knowledge, travailing as much to be delivered from abundance by teaching, as Sir *Philip's* rich nature, and induſtry thirſted to be taught, and manured;

this

this harmony of an humble Hearer to an excellent Teacher, fo equally fitted them both, as out of a naturall defcent both in love, and plenty, the elder grew taken with a net of his own thread, and the younger taught to lift up himfelf by a thread of the fame fpinning; fo as this reverend *Languet*, orderly fequeftred from his feverall Functions under a mighty King, and *Saxonic* the greateft Prince of *Germany*, became a Nurfe of knowledge to this hopefull young Gentleman, and without any other hire, or motive than this fympathy of affections, accompanyed him in the whole courfe of his three years travail. By which example the judicious Reader may fee, that Worth in every Nation finds her Country, Parents, Neighbours, and Friends, yea, and often, with more honour, dearneffe, and advancement in knowledges, than any pedigree of flefhly kindred, will, or can at home raife, or enlarge them unto. Nay to goe yet farther in this private inftance; It may pleafe the Reader to obferve, how the fame
parallel

parallel of worth, in what age, or eftate foever, as it hath power to win, fo hath it likewife abfolute power to keep. Far unlike thofe creations of chance, which hatch other birds egges; and by advancing men out of chance or complement, lofe them again as faft by neglect. Contrary to which, even when diverfity of years, courfes of life, and fortunes, enforced thefe dear Friends to divide, there yet paffed fuch a continuall courfe of intelligence by Letters from one of them to another, as in their loffe (if they be loft) there be buried many delicate images, and differences, between the reall, and large complexions of thofe active times, and the narrow *falves* of this effeminate age: Becaufe in this excellent mould of their friendfhip, the greateft bufineffes of Eftate were fo mixed with the fweet remiffions of ingenuous good will, as men might eafily difcern in them (as unflattering glaffes) that wifdome, and love, in good fpirits have great affinity together. For a farther demonftration, behold even the fame *Languet* (after he was

was sixty six years of age) fashioning himself a journey into *England*, with the Duke *Casimire*, onely to see that excellent Plant of his own polishing. In which loving, and unexpected meeting, I dare confidently affirm, neither side became loser. At the sea they parted, and made many mutuall tears ominous propheciers of their never meeting again.

These little sparks of two large natures I make bold the longer to insist upon, because the youth, life and fortune of this Gentleman were indeed but sparkes of extraordinary greatnesse in him: which for want of clear vent lay concealed, and in a maner smothered up. And again to bring the children of favor, and chance, into an equall ballance of comparison with birth, worth, and education: and therein abruptly to conclude, that God creates those in his certain, and eternall mouldes, out of which he elects for himself; where Kings choose creatures out of *Pandoras* Tun, and so raise up worth, and no worth; friends or enemies at adventure. Therefore

Therefore what marvail can it be, if these *Iacobs*, and *Esaus* strive ambitiously one with another, as well before as after they come out of such erring, and unperfect wombes?

Now from these particular testimonies to goe on with Sir *Philips* life: though he purposed no monuments of books to the world, out of his great harvest of knowledge; yet doe not his Arcadian Romanties live after him, admired by our foure-eyd Criticks? who, howsoever their common end upon common arts be to affect reputation by depraving censure; yet where nature placeth excellencie above envy, there (it seemeth) she subjecteth these carping eyes to wonder, and shewes the judicious reader, how he may be nourished in the delicacy of his own judgement.

For instance; may not the most refined spirits, in the scope of these dead images (even as they are now) finde, that when Soveraign Princes, to play with their own visions, will put off publique action, which is the splendor of Majestie, and unactively charge the managing of
their

their greateſt affaires upon the ſecond-hand faith, and diligence of Deputies, may they not (I ſay) underſtand, that even then they bury themſelves, and their Eſtates in a cloud of contempt, and under it both encourage, and ſhaddow the conſpiracies of ambitious ſubalternes to their falſe endes, I mean the ruine of States and Princes?

Again, where Kingly Parents will ſuffer, or rather force their wives and daughters, to deſcend from the inequality and reſervedneſſe of Princely education, into the contemptible familiarity, and popular freedome of Shepherds; may we not diſcern that even therein they give thoſe Royall birthes warrant, or opportunity, to break over all circles of honor, ſafe-guards to the modeſty of that ſex; and withall make them fraily apt to change the commanding manners of Princely Birth, into the degrading images of ſervile baſeneſſe? Laſtly, where humor takes away this pomp, and *apparatus* from King, Crown, and Scepter, to make fear a Counſellor, and obſcurity a wiſdom; be that King
at

at home what the current, or credit of his former Government, for a while, may keep him: yet he is sure among forrain Princes to be juftly censured as a Princely Shepherd, or Shepherdifh King: which creatures of fcorn feldome fail to become fit facrifices for home-born difcontentments, or ambitious forrain fpirits to undertake, and offer up.

Againe, who fees not the chanceable arrivall of *Euarchus* into *Arcadia*; his unexpected election to the temporary Soveraignty of that State; his fitting in a cloudy feat of judgement, to give fentence (under a mafk of Shepherds) againft his Son, Nephew, Neeces, the immediate fucceffors to that Scepter; and all accufed and condemned of rape, paricide, adulteries, or treafons, by their own Lawes: I fay who fees not, that thefe dark webs of effeminate Princes be dangerous forerunners of innovation, even in a quiet, and equally tempered people? So that if Sir *Philip* had not made the integrity of this forrain King an image of more conftant, pure, and higher ftrain, than nature makes thofe ordinary mouldes,

mouldes, wherein fhe fafhioneth earthly Princes, even this opportunity, and map of defolation prepared for *Euarchus*, wherein he faw all the fucceffors of this Province juftly condemned under his own fentence, would have raifed up fpecious rights, or pretences for new ambition in him; and upon the never-failing pillars of occafion, amafednes of people, and fad offer of glorious novelties, have tempted him to eftablifh this Election for a time, fucceffively, to him and his for ever?

To be fhort, the like, and finer moralities offer themfelves throughout that various, and dainty work of his, for founder judgements to exercife their Spirits in; fo that if the infancie of thefe *Ideas*, determining in the firft generation, yield the ingenuous Reader fuch pleafant & profitable diverfity, both of flowers, and fruits, let him conceive, if this excellent Image-maker had liv'd to finifh, and bring to perfection this extraordinary frame of his own Common-wealth: I meane, the return of *Bafilius*, from his dreames of humor, to the

the honor of his former Eftate; the marriage of the two fifters with the two excellent Princes; their iffue; the warres ftirred up by *Amphialus*; his marriage with *Helena*; their fucceffions; together with the incident Magnificences, pompes of ftate, providences of councells in treaties of peace, or aliance, fummons of warres, and orderly execution of their diforders; I fay, what a large field an active able fpirit fhould have had to walk in, let the advifed Reader conceive with grief. Efpecially if he pleafe to take knowledge, that in all thefe creatures of his making, his intent, and fcope was, to turn the barren Philofophy precepts into pregnant Images of life; and in them, firft on the Monarch's part, lively to reprefent the growth, ftate, and declination of Princes, change of Government, and lawes: viciffitudes of fedition, faction, fucceffion, confederacies, plantations, with all other errors, or alterations in publique affaires. Then again in the fubjects cafe; the ftate of favor, disfavor, profperitie, adverfity, emulation, quarrell, undertaking, retiring, hofpita-
lity,

lity, travail, and all other moodes of private fortunes, or misfortunes. In which traverses (I know) his purpose was to limn out such exact pictures, of every posture in the minde, that any man being forced, in the straines of this life, to pass through any straights, or latitudes of good, or ill fortune, might (as in a glasse) see how to set a good countenance upon all the discountenances of adversitie, and a stay upon the exorbitant smilings of chance.

Now, as I know this was the first project of these workes, rich (like his youth) in the freedome of affections, wit, learning, stile, form, and facilitie, to please others: so must I again (as ingenuously) confess, that when his body declined, and his piercing inward powers were lifted up to a purer Horizon, he then discovered, not onely the imperfection, but vanitie of these shadowes, how daintily soever limned: as seeing that even beauty it self, in all earthly complexions, was more apt to allure men to evill, than to fashion any goodness in them. And from this ground, in that
memorable

memorable teftament of his, he bequeathed no other legacie, but the fire, to this unpolifhed Embrio. From which fate it is onely referved, untill the world hath purged away all her more grofs corruptions.

Again, they that knew him well, will truly confefs, this *Arcadia* of his to be, both in form, and matter, as much inferior to that unbounded fpirit of his, as the induftry and Images of other mens works, are many times raifed above the writers capacities: and befides acknowledge, that howfoever he could not choofe but give them many afperfions of fpirit, and learning from the Father; yet that they were fcribled rather as pamphlets, for entertainment of time, and friends, than any accompt of himfelf to the world. Becaufe if his purpofe had been to leave his memory in books, I am confident, in the right ufe of Logick, Philofophy, Hiftory, and Poëfie, nay even in the moft ingenuous of Mechanicall Arts, he would have fhewed fuch traits of a fearching, and judicious fpirit; as the profeffors of every faculty would have ſtriven no leſs for him, than the ſeaven Cities did to have *Homer* of their Sept. But the truth is: his end was not writing, even while he wrote; nor his knowledge moulded for tables, or ſchooles; but both his wit, and underſtanding bent upon his heart, to make himſelf and others, not in words or opinion, but in life, and action, good and great.

In which Architectonical art he was ſuch a Maſter, with ſo commending, and yet equall waies amongſt men, that wherſoever he went, he was beloved, and obeyed: yea into what Action ſoever he came laſt at the firſt, he became firſt at the laſt: the whole managing of the buſineſs, not by uſurpation, or violence, but (as it were) by right, and acknowledgment, falling into his hands, as into a naturall Center.

By which onely commendable monopolie of alluring, and improving men, looke how the ſunn drawes all windes after it in fair weather: ſo did the influence of this ſpirit draw mens affections and undertakings to depend upon him.

*CHAP.*

## CHAP. II.

Here I am still enforced to bring pregnant evidence from the dead: amongst whom I have found far more liberall contribution to the honor of true worth, than among those which now live; and in the market of selfnesse, traffique new interest by the discredit of old friends: that ancient wisdome of righting enemies, being utterly worn out of date in our modern discipline.

My first instance must come from that worthy Prince of *Orange*, *William* of *Nassau*, with whom this young Gentleman having long kept intelligence by word, and letters, and in affairs of the highest nature that then passed currant upon the stages of *England*, *France*, *Germany*, *Italy*, the low Countries, or *Spaine*, it seemes that this young Gentleman had, by his mutuall freedome, so imprinted the extraordinary merit of his young yeares into the large wisdome, wifdome, and experience of that excellent Prince, as I paffing out of *Germany* into *England*, and having the unexpected honor to finde this Prince in the Town *Delph*, cannot think it unwelcome to defcribe the clothes of this Prince; his pofture of body, and minde, familiarity, and refervednefs, to the ingenuous Reader, that he may fee with what diverfe Characters Princes pleafe, and Govern Cities, Townes, and Peoples.

His uppermoft garment was a gown, yet fuch as (I dare confidently affirm) a mean-born ftudent, in our Innes of Court, would not have been well-pleafed to walk the ftreets in. Unbuttoned his doublet was, and of like precious matter, and form to the other. His waft-coat (which fhewed itfelf under it) not unlike the beft fort of thofe wollen knit ones, which our ordinary watermen row us in. His Company about him, the Burgeffes of that beer-brewing Town: and he fo fellow-like encompaffed with them, as (had I not known his face) no exterior figne of degree, or refervednefs could have difcovered the inequality of

his

his worth or Eftate from that multitude. Notwithftanding I no fooner came to his prefence, but it pleafed him to take knowledge of me. And even upon that (as if it had been a fignall to make a change) his refpect of a ftranger inftantly begat refpect to himfelf in all about him: An outward paffage of inward greatnefs, which in a popular Eftate I thought worth the obferving. Becaufe there, no pedigree but worth could poffibly make a man Prince and no Prince, in a moment, at his own pleafure.

The bufineffes which he then vouchfafed to impart with me were, the dangerous fate which the Crown of *England*, States of *Germany*, and the Low Countries did ftand threatned with, under an ambitious, and conquering Monarch's hand. The main inftance, a fhort defcription of the Spaniards curious affecting to keep the Romans waies, and ends, in all his actions. On the other fide, the clear fymptomes of the Hectique feaver, univerfally then reigning among the Princes of Chriftendome, ordain'd (as he thought) to behold
this

this undermining disease without fear, till it should prove dangerous, nay incurable to them. This active King of *Spain* having put on a mask of conscience, to cover an invisible conjunction between the temporal, and spiritual ambitions, of these two sometimes creeping, sometimes commanding Romish and Spanish Conquerors. The particulars were many, both excellent and enlightning.

As first, the fatall neutrality of *France*, jealous of the Spanish greatness, as already both wrong'd, and threatned by it: and yet their Kings so full of pleasures, and consequently so easily satisfied with the complements of words, treaties, or alliances, and since the fall of the *Sorbonists*, their own exempted Church so absolutely possest, and govern'd by the Jesuits; as through the bewitching liberties, and bondages of Auricular confession, they were rather wrought to rest upon a vain security of reputed strength, than really to hazzard loss, and help themselves by diversion, or assailing.

Again,

Againe, on the Queens part, by the way of queftion, he fuppofed a little neglect in her Princely mildnefs, while fhe did fuffer a Proteftant party, rais'd by God in that great Kingdome of *France*, to be a ballance or counterpeafe to that dangerous *Heptarchy of Spain* (then fcarce vifible, but fince multiplyed to an unrefiftable greatneffe) I say, for fuffering this ftrong and faithfull party (through want of imployment) to fink into it felf, and so unactively (like a Meteor) to vanifh, or fmother out, in vain and idle apparitions. Withall reverently hee demurr'd, whether it were an omiffion in that excellent Ladies Government, or no, by a remiffe looking on, whilft the *Auftrian* afpiring family framed occafion to gain by begging peace, or buying war from the Grand Signior; and both exceeding much to their own ends; In refpect that once in few years, this Emperor made himfelf Generall by it, over all the forces of Chriftendome; and thereby gained the fame of action; trained up his owne Inftruments Martially,

tially, and got credit with his fellow-bordering Princes, through the common Councell, or participation of fear. Befides that in the conclufions of peace, he ever faved a mafs of riches gather'd by Diets, Contributions, Devotions, and Levies for common defence, which out of the ill-accompting hand of war, became (in his Exchequer) Treafure, to terrifie even thofe Chriftian neighbours that did contribute to it. And the more efpecially he infifted upon this: becaufe all thofe crafty Pageants of her enemies were difguifedly acted, even whilft her Majefty had an Agent of extraordinary diligence, worth, and credit with that vaft Eftate of Turkie, into whofe abfolute and imperious fpirit, without any further charge than infufing the jealoufies of competition, thefe practifes among thofe Auftrian ufurpers, might eafily have been interrupted.

Laftly, it pleafed him to queftion yet a greater over-fight in both thefe Kingdoms, *England*, and *France*: Becaufe while their Princes ftood at gaze, as
upon

upon things far off, they ſtill gave way for the Popiſh, and Spaniſh inviſible Arts, and Counſels, to undermine the greatneſs, and freedom both of Secular and Eccleſiaſticall Princes: a mortall ſickneſs in that vaſt body of *Germany*, and by their inſenſible fall, a raiſing up of the houſe of *Austria* many ſteps towards her long affected Monarchy over the Weſt. The ground of which opinion was (as he thought) in reſpect that even the Catholique Princes, and Biſhops themſelves (had their eyes bin well wakened) would never have endured any cloud, or colour of Religion, to have changed their Princely Soveraignties into ſuch a kind of low, and Chaplaine tenure, as ſince they have ſleepily fallen into: but would rather have ſtirred them with many hands, to binde this Miter-ſuperſtition, with the reall cords of truth. And to that end perchance have ſet *Spain* on work with her new, and ill digeſted Conqueſts: her dangerous enemie *Feſs*: her native *Moors*, and *Iews* (ſince craftily tranſported) and ſo probably have troubled
the

the ufurpations both of the *Pope*, and *Spain*, over that well-tempered, though over-zealous, and fuperftitious Region of *Italy*. Thefe, and fuch other particulars, as I had in charge, and did faithfully deliver from him to her Majefty, are fince performed, or perifhed with time, or occafion.

The laft branch was his free expreffing of himfelfe in the honour of Sir *Philip Sidney*, after this manner: That I would firft commend his own humble fervice, with thofe fore-mentioned Ideas to the Queen; and after crave leave of her freely to open his knowledge, and opinion of a Fellow-fervant of his, that (as he heard) lived unimployed under her. With himfelfe he began *ab ovo*, as having been of *Charles* the fift's Privie Counfell, before he was one and twenty years of age: and fince (as the world knew) either an Actor, or at leaft acquainted with the greateft actions, and affairs of *Europe*; and likewife with her greateft men, and minifters of Eftate. In all which feries of time, multitude of things, and perfons, he
protefted

protefted unto mee (and for her fervice) that if he could judge, her Majefty had one of the ripeft, and greateft Counfellors of Eftate in Sir *Philip Sidney*, that at this day lived in *Europe* : to the triall of which hee was pleafed to leave his owne credit engaged, untill her Majefty might pleafe to employ this Gentleman, either amongft her friends or enemies.

At my return into *England*, I performed all his other cōmandments; this that concerned Sir *Philip* (thinking to make the fine-spun threads of Friendfhip more firm between them) I acquainted Sir *Philip* with : not as queftioning, but fully refolved to doe it. Unto which he at the firft fight oppofing, difcharged my faith impawn'd to the Prince of *Orange*, for the delivery of it; as an act only entending his good, and fo to be perform'd, or difpens'd with at his pleafure; yet for my fatisfaction freely added thefe words : firft, that the Qu. had the life it felf daily attending her : and if fhe either did not, or would not value it fo highly, the commendation
of

of that worthy Prince could be no more (at the beſt) than a lively picture of that life, and ſo of far leſſe credit, and eſtimation with her. His next reaſon was, becauſe Princes love not that forrain Powers ſhould have extraordinary intereſt in their Subjects; much leſſe to be taught by them how they ſhould place their own: as arguments either upbraiding ignorance, or lack of large rewarding goodneſs in them.

This Narration I adventure of, to ſhew the clearneſs, and readineſs of this Gentlemans judgement, in all degrees, and offices of life: with this farther teſtimony of him; that after mature deliberation being once reſolved, he never brought any queſtion of change to afflict himſelf with, or perplex the buſineſs; but left the ſucceſs to His will, that governs the blinde proſperities, and unproſperities of Chance; and ſo works out His own ends by the erring frailties of humane reaſon and affection. Laſtly, to manifeſt that theſe were not complements, ſelf-ends, or uſe of each other, according to our modern faſhion
but

but meer ingenuities of fpirit, to which the ancient greatnefs of hearts ever frankly engaged their Fortunes, let Actions, the lawfully begotten children, equall in fpirit, fhape, and complexion to their parents, be teftimonies ever fufficient.

My fecond inftance comes from the Earle of *Leicefter* his unckle, who told me (after Sir *Philips*, and not long before his own death) that when he undertook the government of the Low Countries, he carryed his Nephew over with him, as one amongft the reft, not only defpifing his youth for a Counfellor, but withall bearing a hand over him as a forward young man. Notwithftanding, in fhort time he faw this Sun fo rifen above his Horizon, that both he and all his Stars were glad to fetch light from him. And in the end acknowleged that he held up the honor of his cafual authority by him, whilft he lived, & found reafõ to withdraw himfelf from that burthen, after his death.

My third record is Sir *Francis Walfingham*

*singham* his Father-in-law; that wife, and active Secretarie. This man (as the world knows) upheld both Religion and State, by using a policy wifely mixt with reflexions of either. He had influence in all Countries, & a hand upon all affairs; Yet even this man hath often confessed to my self, that his *Philip* did so far overshoot him in his own Bow, as those friends which at first were Sir *Philip's* for this Secretaries sake, within a while became so fully owned, and possest by Sir *Philip*, as now he held them at the second hand, by his Son-in-laws native courtesie.

This is that true remission of mind, whereof I would gladly have the world take notice from these dead mens ashes: to the end that we might once again see that ingenuity amongst men, which by liberall bearing witnesse to the merits of others, shews they have some true worth of their own; and are not meerly lovers of themselves, without rivals.

*CHAP.*

## CHAP. III.

TO continue this paſſage a little further: I must lift him above the cenſure of Subjects, and give you an account what reſpect, and honour his worth wanne him amongſt the moſt eminent Monarchs of that time. As firſt with that chief, and beſt of Princes, his moſt excellent Majeſty, then King of *Scotland*, to whom his ſervice was affectionately devoted, and from whom he received many pledges of love, and favour.

In like manner, with the late renowned *Henry* of *France*, then of *Navarre*, who having meaſured, and maſtered all the ſpirits in his own Nation, found out this Maſter-ſpirit among us, and uſed him like an equall in nature, and ſo fit for friendſhip with a King.

Again, that gallant Prince *Don John de Auſtria*, Vice-Roy in the Low Countries for *Spain*, when this Gentleman in his

his Embaffage to the Emperor came to kifs his hand, though at the firft, in his Spanifh haughture, he gave him accefs as by defcent to a youth, of grace as to a ftranger, and in particular competition (as he conceived) to an enemy; yet after a while that he had taken his juft altitude, he found himfelf fo ftricken with this extraordinary Planet, that the beholders wondered to fee what ingenuous tribute that brave, and high minded Prince paid to his worth; giving more honour and refpect to this hopefull young Gentleman, than to the Embaffadors of mighty Princes.

But to climb yet a degree higher: In what due eftimation his extraordinary Worth was, even amongft enemies, will appear by his death. When *Mendoza*, a Secretary of many Treafons againft us, acknowledged openly; That howfoever he was glad King *Philip* his Mafter had loft, in a private Gentleman, a dangerous Enemy to his Eftate; yet he could not but lament to fee Chriftendome depriv'd of fo rare a Light in thefe cloudy times; and bewail poor Widdow *England* (fo he term'd term'd her) that having been many years in breeding one eminent fpirit, was in a moment bereaved of him, by the hands of a villain.

Indeed he was a true modell of Worth; A man fit for Conqueft, Plantation, Reformation, or what Action foever is greateft, and hardeft amongft men: Withall, fuch a lover of Mankind, and Goodneffe, that whofoever had any reall parts, in him found comfort, participation, and protection to the uttermoft of his power; like *Zephyrus* he giving life where he blew. The Univerfities abroad, and at home, accompted him a generall *Maecenas* of Learning; Dedicated their Books to him; and communicated every Invention, or Improvement of Knowledge with him. Souldiers honoured him, and were fo honoured by him, as no man thought he marched under the true Banner of *Mars*, that had not obtained Sir *Philip Sidney*'s approbation. Men of Affairs in moft parts of Chriftendome, entertained correfpondency with him. But what fpeak I of thefe, with whom his own waies, and ends did concur? fince (to defcend) his heart,

heart, and capacity were so large, that there was not a cunning Painter, a skilfull Engenier, an excellent Musician, or any other Artificer of extraordinary fame, that made not himself known to this famous Spirit, and found him his true friend without hire; and the common *Rende-vous* of Worth in his time.

 Now let Princes vouchsafe to consider, of what importance it is to the honour of themselves, and their Estates, to have one man of such eminence; not onely as a nourisher of vertue in their Courts, or service; but besides for a reformed Standard, by which even the most humorous persons could not but have a reverend ambition to be tried, and approved currant. This I doe the more confidently affirm, because it will be confessed by all men, that this one man's example, and personall respect, did not onely encourage Learning, and Honour in the Schooles, but brought the affection, and true use thereof both into the Court, and Camp. Nay more, even many Gentlemen excellently learned amongst us, will not deny, but that they affected to
row,

row, and fteer their courfe in his wake. Befides which honour of unequall nature, and education, his very waies in the world, did generally adde reputation to his Prince, and Country, by reftoring amongft us the ancient Majeftie of noble, and true dealing: As a manly wifdome, that can no more be weighed down, by any effeminate craft, than *Hercules* could be overcome by that contemptible Army of Dwarfs. This was it which, I profefs, I loved dearly in him, and ftill fhall be glad to honour in the great men of this time: I mean, that his heart and tongue went both one way, and fo with every one that went with the Truth; as knowing no other kindred, partie, or end.

Above all, he made the Religion he profeffed, the firm Bafis of his life: For this was his judgement (as he often told me) that our true-heartedneffe to the Reformed Religion in the beginning, brought Peace, Safetie, and Freedome to us; concluding, that the wifeft, and beft way, was that of the famous *William* Prince of *Orange*, who never divided the confideration of Eftate from the caufe
of

of Religion, nor gave that sound party occasion to be jealous, or distracted, upon any apparance of safety whatsoever; prudently resolving, that to temporize with the Enemies of our Faith, was but (as among Sea-guls) a strife, not to keep upright, but aloft upon the top of every billow: Which false-heartednesse to God and man, would in the end find it self forsaken of both; as Sir *Philip* conceived. For to this active spirit of his, all depths of the Devill proved but shallow fords; he piercing into mens counsels, and ends, not by their words, oathes, or complements, all barren in that age, but by fathoming their hearts, and powers, by their deeds, and found no wisdome where he found no courage, nor courage without wisdome, nor either without honesty and truth. With which solid, and active reaches of his, I am perswaded, he would have found, or made a way through all the traverses, even of the most weak and irregular times. But it pleased God in this decrepit age of the world, not to restore the image of her
ancient

ancient vigour in him, otherwife than as in a lightning before death.

Neither am I (for my part) fo much in love with this life, nor believe fo little in a better to come, as to complain of God for taking him, and fuch like exorbitant worthynefs from us: fit (as it were by an Oftracifme) to be divided, and not incorporated with our corruptions: yet for the fincere affection I bear to my Prince, and Country, my prayer to God is, that his Worth, and Way may not fatally be buried with him; in refpect, that both before his time, and fince, experience hath publifhed the ufuall difcipline of greatnes to have been tender of it felf onely; making honour a triumph, or rather trophy of defire, fet up in the eyes of Mankind, either to be worfhiped as Idols, or elfe as Rebels to perifh under her glorious oppreffions. Notwithftanding, when the pride of flefh, and power of favour fhall ceafe in thefe by death, or difgrace; what then hath time to regifter, or fame to publifh in thefe great mens names, that will not be
offenfive,

offenfive, or infectious to others? What Pen without blotting can write the ftory of their deeds? Or what Herald blaze their Arms without a blemifh? And as for their counfels and projects, when they come once to light, fhall they not live as noyfome, and loathfomely above ground, as their Authors carkaffes lie in the grave? So as the return of fuch greatnes to the world, and themfelves, can be but private reproach, publique ill example, and a fatall fcorn to the Government they live in. Sir *Philip Sidney* is none of this number; for the greatnefs which he affected was built upon true Worth; efteeming Fame more than Riches, and Noble actions far above Nobility it felf.

## CHAP. IV.

ANd although he never was Magiftrate, nor poffeffed of any fit ftage for eminence to act upon, wherby there is fmall latitude left for comparing

comparing him with those deceased Worthies, that to this day live unenvied in story; Yet can I probably say, that if any supreme Magistracie, or employment, might have shewed forth this Gentlemans Worth, the World should have found him neither a mixt *Lysander*, with unactive goodness to have corrupted indifferent Citizens; nor yet like that gallant Libertine *Sylla*, with a tyrannizing hand, and ill example, to have ordered the dissolute people of *Rome*; much less with that unexperienced *Themistocles*, to have refused, in the seat of Justice, to deale equally between friends and strangers. So that as we say, the abstract name of goodness is great, and generally currant; her nature hard to imitate, and diversly worshipped, according to Zones, complexions, or education; admired by her enemies, yet ill followed by her friends: So I may well say, that this Gentlemans large, yet uniform disposition was every where praised; greater in himself than in the world; yet greater there in fame and honour than many of his superiors;

reverenced

reverenced by forrain Nations in one form, of his own in another; eafily cenfured, hardly imitated; and therefore no received Standard at home, becaufe his induftry, judgement, and affections, perchance feemed too great for the cautious wifdomes of little Monarchies to be fafe in. Notwithftanding, whofoever will be pleafed indifferently to weigh his life, actions, intentions, and death, fhall find he had fo fweetly yoaked fame and confcience together in a large heart, as inequality of worth, or place in him, could not have been other than humble obedience, even to a petty Tyrant of *Sicily*. Befides, this ingenuitie of his nature did fpread it felf fo freely abroad, as who lives that can fay he ever did him harm; whereas there be many living, that may thankfully acknowledge he did them good? Neither was this in him a private, but a publique affection; his chief ends being not Friends, Wife, Children, or himfelf; but above all things the honour of his Maker, and fervice of his Prince, or Country.

Now

Now though his short life, and private fortune, were (as I sayd) no proper stages to act any greatness of good, or evill upon; yet are there (even from these little centers of his) lines to be drawn, not Astronomicall, or imaginary, but reall lineaments, such as infancy is of man's estate; out of which nature often sparkleth brighter rayes in some, than ordinarily appear in the ripeness of many others. For proof wherof, I will pass from the testimonie of brave mens words, to his own deeds. What lights of sounder wisdome can we ascribe to our greatest men of affairs than he shewed in his youth, and first employment, when he was sent by the late *Queen* of famous memory, to condole the death of *Maximilian*, and congratulate the succession of *Rodolph* to the Empire? For under the shadow of this complement between Princes, which sorted better with his youth than his spirit, did he not, to improve that journey, and make it a real service to his Soveraign, procure an Article to be added to his Instructions, which gave him

him scope (as he passed) to salute such *German* Princes, as were interested in the cause of our Religion, or their own native liberty?

And though to negotiate with that long-breathed Nation proves commonly a work in steel, where many stroaks hardly leave any print; yet did this Master *Genius* quickly stir up their cautious, and slow judgements to be sensible of the danger which threatned them hourely, by this fatall conjunction of *Rome's* undermining superstitions, with the commanding forces of *Spain*. And when he had once awaked that confident Nation to look up, he as easily made manifest unto them, that neither their inland seat, vast multitude, confused strength, wealth, nor hollow-sounding Fame could secure their Dominions from the ambition of this brave aspiring Empire; howsoever by the like helps they had formerly bounded the same Roman, and Austrian supremacies. The reasons he alleged were, because the manner of this conjunction was not like the ancient undertakers,

undertakers, who made open war by Proclamation; but craftily (from the infufion of *Rome*) to enter firft by invifible traffique of fouls; filling peoples minds with apparitions of holines, fpecious Rites, Saints, Miracles, inftitutions of new Orders, reformations of old, bleffings of Catholiques, curfings of Heretiques, Thunder-bolts of Excommunication under the authority of their Mother Church. And when by thefe fhadows they had gotten poffeffion of the weak, difcouraged the ftrong, divided the doubtful, and finely lulled inferior powers afleep; as the ancient Romans were wont to tame forrain nations with the name *Socij*; then to follow on with the Spanifh, lefs fpirituall, but more forcible Engines, *viz.* practice, confederacy, faction, money, treaties, leagues of traffique, alliance by marriages, charge of rebellion, war, and all other acts of advantagious power.

Laftly he recalled to their memories, how by this brotherhood in evill (like *Simeon*, and *Levi*) *Rome* and *Spain* had fpilt fo much bloud, as they were juftly
become

become the terror of all Governments; and could now be withstood, or ballanced by no other means, than a general league in Religion: Constantly and truely affirming, that to associate by an uniform bond of conscience, for the protection (as I said) of Religion, and Liberty, would prove a more solid union, and symbolize far better against their Tyrannies, than any Factious combination in policy, league of state, or other traffique of Civill, or Martial humors possibly could do.

To this end did that undertaking spirit lay, or at least revive the foundation of a league between us, and the *German* Princes, which continues firme to this day: The defensive part whereof hath hitherto helped to support the ruines of our Church abroad, and diverted her enemies from the ancient ways of hostility, unto their *Conclave*, and modern undermining Arts. So, that if the offensive part thereof had been as well prosecuted in that true path, which this young *Genius* trod out to us; both the passage for other Princes
over

over the *Alps*, would have been by this time more eafie than *Hanibal's* was; and befides, the firft found of that Drum might happily have reconciled thofe petty dividing Schifmes which reign amongft us; not as fprung from any difference of religious Faith, but mifty Opinion; and accordingly moulded firft upon the Desks of bufie idle Lecturers, then blown abroad to our difadvantage by a fwarm of Popifh Inftruments, rather Jefuits than Chriftians; and to their ends moft dangeroufly overfpreading the world, for want of a confident Moderator. This (I fay) was the firft prize which did enfranchife this Mafter Spirit into the myfteries, and affairs of State.

## CHAP. V.

THe next doubtfull Stage hee had to act upon (howfoever it may feem private) was grounded upon a publique and fpecious propofition
of

of marriage, between the late famous Queen, and the Duke of *Aniou*. With which Current, although he faw the great, and wife men of the time fuddainly carryed down, and every one fifhing to catch the Queens humor in it; yet when he confidered the difference of years, perfon, education, ftate, and religion between them; and then called to minde the fuccefs of our former alliances with the *French*: he found many reafons to make queftion whether it would prove Poetical, or reall on their part? And if reall; yet whether the ballance fwayed not unequally, by adding much to them, and little to his Soveraign? The Dukes greatnefs being onely name, and poffibility; and both thefe either to wither, or be maintained at her coft. Her ftate again in hand; and though Royally fufficient to fatisfie that Queens Princely and moderate defires, or expences, yet perchance inferior to bear out thofe mixt defignes, into which his ambition, or neceffities might entife, or draw her.

Befides, the marriage of K. *Philip*, to Q. *Mary* her fifter, was yet fo frefh in memory,

memory, with the many inconveniences of it, as by comparing and paralleling thefe together, he found credible inftances to conclude, neither of thefe forrain alliances could prove fafe for this Kingdom. Becaufe in her marriage with *Spain*, though both Princes continuing under the obedience of the *Roman* Church, neither their confciences, nor their peoples could fuffer any fear of tumult, or imputation by change of faith; Yet was the winning of St. *Quintins*, with the lofs of *Calice*, and the carrying away of our money to forrain ends, odious univerfally; the *Spanifh* pride incompatible; their advantagious delayes fufpicious; and their fhort reign here felt to be a kinde of exhaufting tax upon the whole Nation.

Befides, he difcerned how this great Monarch countenanced with our Forces by fea, and land, might, and did ufe this addition of her ftrength to transform his Low-Countrey Dukedomes, fall'n to him by defcent, into the nature of a foveraign conqueft; and fo by conjoyning their Dominion, and Forces by
Sea,

Sea, to his large Empires, and Armies upon the Mayn, would probably enforce all abſolute Princes to acknowledg ſubjection to him before their time. And for our Kingdome, beſides that this King then meant to uſe it as a forge, to faſhion all his ſoveraign deſignes in; had he not (except ſome bely him) a fore-running hand in the change of Religion after King *Edwards* death? And had he not (even in that change) ſo maſtered us in our own Church, by his Chaplain and Conclave of *Rome*, that both theſe carried all their courſes byaced to his ends, as to an elder brother, who had more abundant degrees of wealth, and honour to return them? ſo as every body (that devoted Queen excepted) foreſaw we muſt ſuddenly have been compelled to wear his livery, and ſerve his ends; or elſe to live like children neglected, or disfavoured by our holy Mother.

Again, for our temporall Government; was not his influence (except report belie him) as well in paſſing many ſharp lawes, and heavy executions of them with more

ſtrange

ſtrange Councels; as faſhioning our leagues both of peace, and traffique to his conquering ends? All theſe together, with that Maſter prize of his playing, when under colour of piety, he ſtirred up in that wel-affected Queen a purpoſe of reſtoring thoſe temporalities to the Church, which by the fall of Abbies, were long before diſperſed among the Nobility, Gentry, and people of this Kingdome: all theſe (as he ſaid) did clearly ſhew, that this ambitious King had an intent of moulding us to his uſe, even by diſtracting us amongſt our ſelves.

Nevertheleſſe, to give him the honor of worldly wiſedom, I dare aver, he had no hope of bringing theſe curious aſſumptions to paſs; but rather did caſt them out, as founding lines, to fathome the depths of peoples mindes; and with particular fear, and diſtraction in the owners, to raiſe a generall diſtaſt in all men againſt the Government. Now, if we may judge the future by what is paſt, his ſcope in all theſe particulars could be no other, but when our inward waters had been throughly troubled, then to poſſeſs

possess this diversly diseas'd Estate with certain poëticall titles of his own, devised long before, and since published by *Dolman*, to the end, that under the shadow of such clouds, he might work upon the next heir; and so cast a chance for all our goodes, lives, and liberties with little interruption. These, and such like, were the groundes which moved Sir *Philip* to compare the past, and present consequence of our Marriage with either of these Crowns together.

And though in danger of subjection he did confess our aliance with the French to be lesse unequall; yet even in that, he foresaw, diversitie of Religion would first give scandall to both; and in progress, prove fatall of necessity to one side. Because the weaker sect here, being fortified by strong parties abroad, and a husbands name at home, must necessarily have brought the native Soveraign under a kinde of Covert Baron, and thereby forced her Majesty, either to lose the freedom, and conscience of a good Christian, the honor
of

of an excellent Prince, or the private reputation of an obedient Wife. Neither could that excellent Lady (as he, and that time conceived) with thefe, or any other cautions, have countermined the mines of practice, whereby (it is probable) this Prince would have endeavoured to fteal change of Religion into her Kingdom.

1. As firft, by cavelling at the Authors, and Fathers that upheld her Church.

2. Then by difgracing her moft zealous Minifters, through afperfions caft upon their perfons, and advancing indifferent fpirits, whofe God is this world, the Court their heaven, and confequently their ends, to biace God's immortall truth to the fantafies of mortall Princes.

3. By the fubtile latitude of fchool-diftinctions, publiquely edging nearer the holy mother Church; and therein firft waving, then founding the peoples mindes; if not with abrupt, and fpirit-fall'n tolleration, yet with that invifible web of connivencie, which is a fnare to entangle

entangle great, or little flies, at the will of power.

4. By a Princely licentiousnesse in behaviour, and conference, fashioning atheisme among her Subjects: as knowing that in confusion of thoughts, he might the more easilie raise up superstitious idolatry: which crafty Image of his, with all the nice lineaments belonging to it, was the more credible, in respect the French have scornfully affirm'd one chief branch of our Princes prerogatives to be, the carying of their peoples consciences which way they list. An absolutenes the more dangerous to their subjects freedom, because they bring these changes to pass (as the French say) under the safe conduct of our earth-eyd common law; and thereby make change legally safe, and constancie in the truth exceeding dangerous.

5. By a publique decrying of our ancient Customes, and Statutes; and from that ground, giving Proclamations a Royall vigor in moulding of pleas, pulpits and Parliaments, after the pattern

tern of their own, and some other forain Nations; which in our Government is a confusion, almost as fatall as the confusion of tongues.

6. By employing no instruments among the people, but such as devise to sheer them with taxes, ransome them with fines, draw in bondage under colour of obedience, and (like Frenchified *Empsons*, and *Dudlies*) bring the English people to the povertie of the French Peasants, onely to fill up a *Danaus* sive of prodigality, and thereby to secure the old age of Tyranny from that which is never old: I mean, danger of popular inundations.

7. To lift up Monarchie above her ancient legall Circles, by banishing all free spirits, and faithfull Patriots, with a kinde of shaddowed Ostracisme, till the *Ideas* of native freedom should be utterly forgotten; and then (by the pattern of their own Duke of *Guise*) so to encourage a multitude of impoverishing impositions upon the people, as he might become the head of all discontentedness; and under the envy of that art, stir them up

up to depose their naturall annointed Soveraign.

8. When he had thus metamorphosed our moderate form of Monarchie into a precipitate absolutenefs; and therein shaken all Leagues offensive or defensive between us, the Kings of *Denmark*, and *Sweden*, the free Princes of *Germany*, the poor oppressed soules of *France*, the steady subsisting *Hanses*; and lastly weakned that league of Religion, and traffique, which with prosperous succefs hath continued long between us, and the *Netherlanders*; then (I say) must his next project have been, either abusively to entise, or through fear enforce this excellent Lady, to countenance his overgrown party abroad, by suffering the same sect to multiply here at home, till she should too late discover a necessity, either of changing her faith, hazarding her Crown, or at least holding it at the joint courtesie of that ambitious Roman Conclave, or encreasing Monarchie of *Spain*. A Scepter, and Miter, whose conjunction bringes forth boundlefs freedom to themselves, and begets a
narrow

narrow fervitude upon all other Nations, that by furprife of wit, or power become fubject to them.

9. Befides, in the practice of this Marriage, he forefaw, and prophefied, that the very firft breach of Gods ordinance, in matching herfelf with a Prince of a diverfe faith, would infallibly carry with it fome piece of the rending deftiny, which *Solomon*, and thofe other Princes juftly felt, for having ventured to weigh the immortall wifdom in even fcales, with mortall conveniency or inconveniency.

10. The next ftep muft infallibly have been (as he conceived) with our fhipping to difturb or beleaguer the *Netherlanders* by Sea, under colour, or pretence of honor unfeafonably taken, even when the horfe and foot of *France* fhould threaten their fubfiftence by land; and therby (in this period of extremity) conftrain that active people to run headlong into one of thefe three defperate courfes, *viz.* Either to fly for protection to the Flower-de-Luce, with whom they join in continent; Or precipitately fubmit

their

their necks to the yoking Cittadells of *Spain*, againſt whoſe inquiſitions, and uſurpations upon their Conſciences, and Liberties, ſo much money, and bloud had been ſhed, and conſumed already; Or elſe unnaturally to turn Pirates, and ſo become enemies to that trade, by which they and their friends have reciprocally gotten, and given ſo much proſperity. The choice or compariſon of which miſchiefes to them, and us, he briefly laid before me, in this manner.

Firſt, that if they ſhould incorporate with *France*, the *Netherlands* manufactures, induſtry, trade, and ſhipping, would add much to that Monarchie, both in peace, and war: The naturall riches of the French having been hitherto either kept barrain at home, or barrainly tranſported abroad, for lack of the true uſe of trade, ſhipping, exchange, and ſuch other myſteries as multiply native wealth; by improving their man-hood at home, and giving formes both to domeſtique, and forrain materialls; which defect (as he ſaid) being now abundantly to be ſupplied, by this conjunction with the
*Netherlands*,

*Netherlands*, would in a little time, not onely puff up that active Commonwealth with unquiet pride, but awake the ſtirring French to feel this addition to their own ſtrengths; and ſo make them become dangerous neighbours by incurſion or invaſion to the Baltique Sea; many waies prejudice to the mutuall traffique between *Italy*, the *Germans*, and *England*; and conſequently a terror to all others, that by land, or Sea confine upon them, yea and apt enough once in a year, to try their fortune with that growing Monarch of *Spain*, for his Indian treaſure.

2. On the other side; if any ſtricter league ſhould come to paſs between thoſe adventurous French Spirits, and the ſolid counſells of *Spaine*; and ſo through fear, ſcorn, or any other deſperate apparances force the *Netherlands* into a precipitate, but ſteady ſubjection of that Spaniſh Monarchie; then he willed me to obſerve, how this fearfull union of Earth, and Sea, having eſcaped the petty Monarches of *Europe*, would in all probability, conſtrain them to play
after-games

after-games for their own Estates. Because these two potent Navies (his and the *Netherland's*) being thus added to his invincible Armies by land, would soon (as he thought) compell that head of holy mother Church, whose best use for many yeares had been (by ballancing these two Emperiall greatnesses one with another) to secure inferior Princes: would (as I said) soon enforce that sacred Mother-head to shelter her self under the wings of this Emperiall Eagle, and so absolutely quit her Miter-supremacie; or at least become Chaplain to this suppressing, or supporting Conqueror.

Besides, in this fatall probability he discovered the great difference between the wisdom of quiet Princes, in their moderate desires of subsistence, from the large, and hazardous counsells of undertaking Monarches; whose ends are onely to make force the umpier of right, and by that inequality become Soveraign Lords (without any other title) over equalls and inferiors.

3. Now for this third point, of constraining

ſtraining this oppreſſed, yet active *Netherland* people to become Pirates: he willed me in the examples of time paſt to obſerve, how much *Scirpalus* did annoy the Grecians; *Sextus Pompeius* the Romans, even in their greatneſs; and in the modern, *Fluſhing, Dunkerk, Rochell* and *Algiers.* Inferring withall, that this people, which had ſo long proſpered upon the rich materialls of all Nations, by the two large ſpreading armes of manufacture, and traffique, could not poſſibly be forced at once to leave this habit: but would rather deſperately adventure to maintain theſe enriching ſtrengthes of marriners, ſouldiers, and ſhipping of their own, with becomming a Rende-vous for the ſwarm of diſcontented ſubjects univerſally; inviting them with hope of ſpoil, and by that inheritance, to try whether the world were ready to examine her old foundations of freedom, in the ſpecious, and flattering regions of change, and Powers encrochments?

Laſtly, beſides this uneven ballance of State; the very reflexion of ſcorn between

between age, and youth; her comeli-
nefs, his difadvantage that way; the
exceffive charge by continuall refort of
the French hither; danger of change
for the worfe; her reall native States
and riches made fubject to forrain humors; little hope of fucceffion, and if
any, then *France* affured to become the
feat, and *England* the Province; children, or no children, misfortune, or un-
certainty: Thefe (I fay) and fuch like
threatning probabilities made him joyn
with the weaker party, and oppofe this
torrent; even while the French faction
reigning had caft afperfions upon his
Uncle of *Leicefter*, and made him, like
a wife man (under colour of taking
phyfick) voluntarily become prifoner in
his chamber.

## CHAP. VI.

THus ftood the ftate of things
then: And if any judicious Reader
fhall afk, Whether it were not an
error, and a dangerous one, for Sir
*Philip*

*Philip* being neither Magiftrate nor Counfellor, to oppofe himfelf againft his Soveraigns pleafure in things indifferent? I muft anfwer, That his worth, truth, favour, and fincerity of heart, together with his reall manner of proceeding in it, were his privileges. Becaufe this Gentlemans courfe in this great bufinefs was, not by murmur among equals, or inferiours, to detract from Princes; or by a mutinous kind of bemoaning error, to ftir up ill affections in their minds, whofe beft thoughts could do him no good; but by a due addrefs of his humble reafons to the *Queen* her felf, to whom the appeal was proper. So that although he found a fweet ftream of Soveraign humors in that well-tempered Lady, to run againft him, yet found he fafety in her felf, againft that felfnefs which appeared to threaten him in her: For this happily born and bred Princefs was not (fubject-like) apt to conftrue things reverently done in the worft fenfe; but rather with the fpirit of annointed Greatnefs (as created to reign equally over

over frail and ftrong) more defirous to find waies to fafhion her people, than colours, or caufes to punifh them.

Laftly, to prove nothing can be wife, that is not really honeft; every man of that time, and confequently of all times may know, that if he fhould have ufed the fame freedome among the Grandees of Court (their profeffion being not commonly to difpute Princes purpofes for truths fake, but fecond their humours to govern their Kingdomes by them) he muft infallibly have found Worth, Juftice, and Duty lookt upon with no other eyes but *Lamia's*; and fo have been ftained by that reigning faction, which in all Courts allows no faith currant to a Soveraign, that hath not paft the feal of their practifing corporation.

Thus ftood the Court at that time; and thus ftood this ingenuous fpirit in it. If dangeroufly in mens opinions who are curious of the prefent, and in it rather to doe craftily, than well: Yet, I fay, that Princely heart of hers was a Sanctuary unto him; And as for the

the people, in whom many times the lasting images of Worth are preferred before the temporary visions of art, or favour, he could not fear to suffer any thing there, which would not prove a kind of Trophy to him. So that howsoever he seemed to stand alone, yet he stood upright; kept his access to her Majesty as before; a liberall conversation with the *French*, reverenced amongst the worthiest of them for himselfe, and born in too strong a fortification of nature for the less worthy to abbord, either with question, familiarity, or scorn.

In this freedome, even while the greatest spirits, and Estates seemed hood-winkt, or blind; and the inferior sort of men made captive by hope, fear, ignorance; did he enjoy the freedome of his thoughts, with all recreations worthy of them.

And in this freedome of heart being one day at Tennis, a Peer of this Realm, born great, greater by alliance, and superlative in the Princes favour, abruptly came into the Tennis-Court;
and

and speaking out of these three paramount authorities, he forgot to entreat that, which he could not legally command. When by the encounter of a steady object, finding unrespectiveness in himself (though a great Lord) not respected by this Princely spirit, he grew to expostulate more roughly. The returns of which stile comming still from an understanding heart, that knew what was due to it self, and what it ought to others, seemed (through the mists of my Lords passions, swoln with the winde of his faction then reigning) to provoke in yeelding. Whereby, the lesse amazement, or confusion of thoughts he stirred up in Sir *Philip*, the more shadowes this great Lords own mind was possessed with: till at last with rage (which is ever ill-disciplin'd) he commands them to depart the Court. To this Sir *Philip* temperately answers; that if his Lordship had been pleased to express desire in milder Characters, perchance he might have led out those, that he should now find would not be driven out with any scourge of fury.

This

This anfwer (like a Bellows) blowing up the fparks of excefs already kindled, made my Lord fcornfully call Sir *Philip* by the name of Puppy. In which progrefs of heat, as the tempeft grew more and more vehement within, fo did their hearts breath out their perturbations in a more loud and fhrill accent. The *French* Commiffioners unfortunately had that day audience, in thofe private Galleries, whofe windows looked into the Tennis-Court. They inftantly drew all to this tumult: every fort of quarrels forting well with their humors, efpecially this. Which Sir *Philip* perceiving, and rifing with inward ftrength, by the profpect of a mighty faction againft him; asked my Lord, with a loud voice, that which he heard clearly enough before. Who (like an Echo, that ftill multiplies by reflexions) repeated this Epithet of Puppy the fecond time. Sir *Philip* refolving in one anfwer to conclude both the attentive hearers, and paffionate actor, gave my Lord a Lie, impoffible (as he averred) to be retorted; in refpect all the world knows,

knows, Puppies are gotten by Dogs, and Children by men.

Hereupon thofe glorious inequalities of Fortune in his Lordfhip were put to a kinde of paufe, by a precious inequality of nature in this Gentleman. So that they both ftood filent a while, —like a dumb fhew in a Tragedy; till Sir *Philip* fenfible of his own wrong, the forrain, and factious fpirits that attended; and yet, even in this queftion between him, and his fuperior, tender to his Countries honour; with fome words of fharp accent, led the way abruptly out of the Tennis-Court; as if fo unexpected an accident were not fit to be decided any farther in that place. Whereof the great Lord making another fenfe, continues his play, without any advantage of reputation; as by the ftandard of humours in thofe times it was conceived.

A day Sir *Philip* remains in fufpenfe, when hearing nothing of, or from the Lord, he fends a Gentleman of worth to awake him out of his trance; wherein the *French* would affuredly think any
paufe,

paufe, if not death, yet a lethargy of true honour in both. This ftirred a refolution in his Lordlhip to fend Sir *Philip* a Challenge. Notwithftanding, thefe thoughts in the great Lord wandred fo long between glory, anger, and inequality of ftate, as the Lords of her Majefties Counfell took notice of the differences, commanded peace, and laboured a reconciliation between them. But needlefly in one refpect, and bootlefly in another. The great Lord being (as it fhould feem) either not hafty to adventure many inequalities againft one, or inwardly fatisfied with the progrefs of his own Acts: Sir *Philip* on the other fide confident, he neither had nor would lofe, or let fall any thing of his right. Which her Majefties Counfell quickly perceiving, recommended this work to her felf.

The Queen, who faw that by the lofs, or difgrace of either, fhe could gain nothing, prefently undertakes Sir *Philip*; and (like an excellent Monarch) lays before him the difference in degree between Earls, and Gentlemen; the re- fpect spect inferiors ought to their superiors; and the necessity in Princes to maintain their own creations, as degrees descending between the peoples licentiousness, and the anoynted Soveraignty of Crowns: how the Gentlemans neglect of the Nobility taught the Peasant to insult upon both.

Whereunto Sir *Philip*, with such reverence as became him, replyed: First, that place was never intended for privilege to wrong: witness her self, who how Soveraign soever she were by Throne, Birth, Education, and Nature; yet was she content to cast her own affections into the same moulds her Subjects did, and govern all her rights by their Laws. Again, he besought her Majesty to consider, that although he were a great Lord by birth, alliance, and grace; yet hee was no Lord over him: and therefore the difference of degrees between free men, could not challenge any other homage than precedency. And by her Fathers Act (to make a Princely wisdom become the more familiar) he did instance the

Government

Government of K. *Henry* the eighth, who gave the Gentry free, and fafe appeal to his feet, againſt the oppreſſion of the Grandees; and found it wifdome, by the ſtronger corporation in number, to keep down the greater in power: inferring elfe, that if they ſhould unite, the over-grown might be tempted, by ſtill coveting more, to fall (as the Angels did) by affecting equality with their Maker.

This conſtant tenor of truth he took upon him; which as a chief duty in all creatures, both to themſelves, & the ſoveraignty above them, protected this Gentleman (though he obeyed not) from the difpleafure of his Soveraign. Wherein he left an authentical prefident to after ages, that howſoever tyrants allow of no fcope, ſtamp, or ſtandard, but their own will; yet w<sup>th</sup> Princes there is a latitude for fubjects to referve native, & legall freedom, by paying hūble tribute in manner, though not in matter, to them.

*CHAP.*

## CHAP. VII.

THE next ſtep which he intended into the world, was an expedition of his own projecting; wherein he faſhioned the whole body, with purpoſe to become head of it himſelf. I mean the laſt employment but one of Sir *Francis Drake* to the Weſt Indies. Which journey, as the ſcope of it was mixt both of ſea, and land ſervice; ſo had it accordingly diſtinct Officers, & Commanders, choſen by Sir *Philip* out of the ableſt Governors of thoſe Martiall times. The project was contrived between themſelves in this manner; that both ſhould equally be Governours, when they had left the ſhore of *England*; but while things were a preparing at home, Sir *Fran.* was to bear the name, and ‧by the credit of Sir *Phil.* have all particulars abundantly ſupplyed.

The reaſon of which ſecret carriage was, the impoſſibility for Sir *Philip* to win

win the Queen, or Government (out of the value which they rated his worth at) to difpenfe with an employment for him fo remote, and of fo hazardous a nature. Befides his credit, and reputation with the State lay not that way. So as our provident Magiftrates expecting a Prentifhip more ferioufly in Martial, than Mechanical actions; and therein meafuring all men by one rule; would (as Sir *Philip* thought) not eafily believe his unexperience equall for a defigne of fo many divers, and dangerous paffages: howfoever wife men, even in the moft active times have determined this art of Government, to be rather a riches of nature, than any proper fruit of induftry, or education. This (as I faid) was one reafon, why Sir *Philip* did cover that glorious enterprize with a cloud. Another was, becaufe in the doing, while it paft unknown, he knew it would pafs without interruption; and when it was done, prefumed the fuccefs would put envy and all her agents to filence.

On the other fide Sir *Francis* found that

that Sir *Philip's* friends, with the influence of his excellent inward powers, would add both weight, and fashion to his ambition; and consequently either with, or without Sir *Philip's* company, yeeld unexpected ease, and honor to him in this voiage.

Upon these two divers Counsels they treat confidently together; the preparations go on with a large hand amongst our Governors; nothing is denyed Sir *Francis* that both their propounding hearts could demand. To make which expedition of less difficulty, they kept the particular of this plot more secret than it was possible for them to keep the generall preparations of so great a journey; hoping that while the *Spaniard* should be forced to arm every where against them, he could not any where be so royally provided to defend himself, but they might land without any great impediment.

In these termes Sir *Francis* departs for *Plimouth* with his ships; vowed and resolved that when he staid for nothing but for a wind, the watch word should

should come post for Sir *Philip*. The time of the year made haste away, & Sr *Francis* to follow it, either made more haste than needed, or at least seemed to make more than really he did. Notwithstanding, as I dare aver that in his own element he was industrous; so dare I not condemn his affections in this misprision of time. Howsoever a letter comes post for Sir *Philip*, as if the whole fleet stayed onely for him, and the wind. In the meanseason the State hath intelligence that *Don Antonio* was at sea for *England*, and resolved to land at *Plimouth*. Sir *Philip* turning occasion into wisdome, puts himself into the imployment of conducting up this King; and under that veil leaves the Court without suspicion; over-shoots his father-in-law then Secretary of Estate in his own bow; comes to *Plimmouth*; was feasted the first night by Sir *Francis*, with a great deale of outward Pomp and complement.

Yet I that had the honor as of being bred with him from his youth; so now (by his own choice of all *England*) to be
his

his loving, and beloved *Achates* in this journey, obferving the countenance of this gallant mariner more exactly than Sir *Philips* leifure ferved him to doe; after we were laid in bed, acquainted him with my obfervation of the difcountenance, and depreffion which appeared in Sir *Francis*; as if our coming were both beyond his expectation, and defire. Neverthelesse that ingenuous fpirit of Sir *Philip's*, though apt to give me credit, yet not apt to difcredit others, made him fufpend his own, & labor to change, or qualifie my judgement; Till within fome few daies after, finding the fhippes neither ready according to promife, nor poffibly to be made ready in many daies; and withall obferving fome fparcks of falfe fire, breaking out unawares from his yoke-fellow daily; It pleafed him (in the freedom of our friendfhip) to return me my own ftock, with intereft.

All this while *Don Antonio* landes not; the fleet feemed to us (like the weary paffengers Inn) ftill to goe further from our defires; letters came from the
Court

Court to haften it away: it may be the leaden feet, and nimble thoughts of Sir *Francis* wrought in the day, and unwrought by night; while he watched an opportunity to difcover us, without being difcovered.

For within a few daies after a poft fteales up to the Court, upon whofe arrivall an Alarum is prefently taken: meffengers fent away to ftay us, or if we refufed, to ftay the whole Fleet. Notwithftanding this firft *Mercury*, his errand being partly advertifed to Sir *Philip* beforehand, was intercepted upon the way; his letters taken from him by two refolute fouldiers in Marriners apparell; brought inftantly to Sir *Philip*, opened, and read. The contents as welcome as Bulls of excommunication to the fuperftitious Romanift, when they enjoyn him either to forfake his right, or his holy Mother-Church, yet did he fit this firft proceffe, without noife, or anfwer.

The next was a more Imperiall Mandate, carefully conveyed, and delivered to himfelf by a Peer of this Realm; carrying

carrying with it in the one hand grace, the other thunder. The grace was an offer of an inftant imployment under his Unckle, then going Generall into the Low-Countries; Againft which although he would gladly have demurred; yet the confluence of reafon, tranfcendencie of Power, fear of ftaying the whole Fleet, made him inftantly facrifife all thefe felfneffes to the duty of obedience.

Wherein how unwillingly foever he yeelded up his knowledge, affections, publique and private endes in that journey; yet did he act this force in a gallant fafhion. Opens his referved ends to the Generall; encourageth the whole Army with promife of his uttermoft affiftance; faves Sir *Francis Drake* from blaftings of Court, to keep up his reputation amongft thofe companies which he was prefently to command; cleareth the dafeled eyes of that Army, by fhewing them, how even in that forrain imployment, which took himfelf from them, the Queen had engaged herfelf more waies than one againft the
Spaniards

Spaniards ambition: fo as there was no probability of taking away her Princely hand from fuch a well-ballanced work of her own.

Neverthelefle as the Limmes of *Venus* picture, how perfectly foever began, and left by *Apelles*, yet after his death proved impoffible to finifh: fo that *Heroicall* defign of invading, and pofleffing *America*, how exactly foever projected, and digefted in every minute by Sir *Philip*, did yet prove impoffible to be well acted by any other mans fpirit than his own; how fufficient foever his affociate were in all parts of navigation; whereby the fuccefs of this journey fell out to be rather fortunate in wealth, than honor.

Whereupon, when Sir *Philip* found this, and many other of his large, and fincere refolutions imprifoned within the pleights of their fortunes, that mixed good, and evill together unequally; and withall difcerned, how the idle-cenfuring faction at home had won ground of the active adventures abroad; then did this double depreffion both of
things,

things, and men, lift up his active spirit into an universall prospect of time, States, and things: and in them made him consider, what possibility there was for him, that had no delight to rest idle at home, of repropounding some other forrain enterprise, probable, and fit to invite that excellent Princesses minde, and moderate Government, to take hold off. The placing of his thoughts upon which high pinnacle, layd the present Map of the Christian world underneath him.

## CHAP. VIII.

IN which view, nature guiding his eyes, first to his Native Country, he found greatness of worth, and place, counterpoysed there by the arts of power, and favor. The stiring spirits sent abroad as fewell, to keep the flame far off: and the effeminate made judges of danger which they fear, and honor which they understand not.

The

The people (by difpofition of the clime) valiant, and multiplying, apt indifferently to corrupt with peace, or refine with action; and therefore to be kept from ruft, or mutiny, by no meanes better than by forrain employments: His opinion being that *Ilanders* have the air and waters fo diverfly moving about them, as neither peace, nor war, can long be welcome to their humors, which muft therefore be govern'd by the active, and yet fteady hand of authority. Befides he obferved the Sea to have fo naturall a Sympathie, with the complexions of them fhe invirons, as be it in traffique, piracie, or war, they are indifferent to wander upon that element; and for the moft part apter to follow undertaking chance, than any fetled endes in a Marchant-traffique.

Now for the bleffed *Lady* which then governed over us: how equall foever fhe were in her happy creation for peace, or war, and her people (as I have fhewed) humble to follow her will in either, yet becaufe fhe refolved to keep within the *Decorum* of her fex, fhe fhewed herfelf
more

more ambitious of ballancing neighbor Princes from invading one another, than under any pretence of title, or revenge, apt to queſtion or conquer upon forrain Princes poſſeſſions. And though this moderate courſe carried her into a defenſive war, which commonly falls out rather to be an impoveriſhing of enemies, than any meanes to enrich, or diſcipline their Eſtates that undertake it; yet could not all the rackes of loſs, injury, or terror, ſtir this excellent *Lady* into any further degree of offenſive war, than onely the keeping of her Navy abroad, to interrupt the ſafe-comming home of his *Indian* Fleet, and hinder the proviſion, contracted for in all parts of *Europe*, to furniſh another invincible Navy, wherewith he purpoſed to beſiege the world, and therein (as his firſt ſtep) her divided Kingdomes.

On the other ſide, in his ſurvay of forrain Nations, he obſerved a fatall paſſiveneſſe generally currant, by reaſon of ſtrange inequalities between little humors and great fortunes in the preſent *Princes* reigning.

Amongſt

Amongst whom for the first object *Henry* the third of *France* appeares to him in the likeness of a good Master, rather than a great King; buried in his pleasures, his Crown demain exhausted, impositions multiplyed, the people light, the Nobility prone to move, and consequently his Country apt, through scorn of his effeminate Vices, either to become a prey for the strongest undertaker, or else to be Cantonized by selfdivision. In both which possible disasters, their native wealth, and variety of objects, perchance have made both King, and people (howsoever confusedly erring) yet to live secured by the providence of chance.

Again, he saw the vast body of the Empire resting (as in a dream) upon an immoveable centre of self-greatness; and under this false assumpsit, to have laid the bridle on the neck of the Emperor, to work them artificially, with a gentle, or steady hand, to his own will.

And to confirm, and multiply this clowdy danger, he discerned how that creeping

creeping Monarchie of *Rome* (by her Arch-inftruments the Iefuits) had already planted fine Schooles of ferving humanity in diverfe of their reformed Cities: intending fo to tempt this welbelieving people, with that old forbidden tree of knowledge, as they might fin desperately againft their own Eftates, before they knew it.

The like mift thefe crafty mift-raifers intented (as he thought) to caft over that well-united fabrick of the *Hanfes*: whofe endes being meerly wealth, and their feats invironed on every fide with active, and powerfull neighbors, would (in all probability) make them as jealous of abfolute Princes in profperity, as zealous in diftrefs to feek protection under them. So that they being at this time grown mighty by combination, if they fhould be neglected, would prove apt, and able to fway the ballance unequally to the endes of the ftronger.

Befides, he difcerned yet a greater, and more malignant afpect from that fpreading Monarchie of *Spain*; which abfolutely commanding the houfe of
*Auftria*,

*Auſtria*, governing the *Conclave*, and having gotten, or affecting to get a commanding intelligence over theſe Cities; would ſoon multiply unavoidable danger, both to themſelves, and us, by mixing the temporall, and ſpirituall ſword, to their crafty conquering ends.

Nay more; how upon the ſame foundation they had begunne yet a more dangerous party, even amongſt the German Princes themſelves; by adding to the fatall oppoſition of Religion between them, the hopes, feares, jealouſie, temptations of reward, or loſs, with all the unnaturall ſeeds of diviſion; which might make them, through theſe confuſed threatnings, and enticements, to become an eaſie prey for the Spaniards watchfull, unſatiable, and much promiſing ambition.

He likewiſe obſerved *Battorie*, that gallant man, but dangerouſly aſpiring King of *Poland*, to be happily peiſed by the ancient competition between him, and his Nobility, and as buſie to encroch upon their Marches, and add more to his own limited Soveraignty, as they were to draw down thofe few prerogatives it had, into that well mixt, and ballanced *Ariftocracie* of theirs.

*Denmark*, howfoever by the opportunity, and narrownefs of his Sound, reftrained to the selfnefs of profit; yet by difcipline, and feat, able to fecond an active undertaker with fhipping, money, &c. But too wife, with thefe ftrengths to help any forrain Prince to become Emperor over himfelf, or otherwife to entangle his Eftate offenfively, or defenfively in common Actions.

The *Sweden* environed, or rather imprifoned with great and dangerous neighbours, and enemies. The *Polack* pretending Title to his Kingdom, and with a continuall claim by fword, inforceing him to a perpetuall defenfive charge. The King of *Denmark* being unfafe to him upon every occafion, by ill neighbourhood among active Princes. And laftly, the barbarous *Mofcovite*, onely quiet through his own diftreffe, and oppreffions elfe-where. So as like a Prince thus ftrictly invironed, the King

King of *Sweden* could not (among Princes) stand as any pregnant place of exorbitant help, or terror; otherwise than by money.

The *Switzers* swoln with equality; divided at home; enemies, yet servants to Monarchies; not easily oppressed, in the opinion of those times; nor able to doe any thing of note alone: and so a dangerous body for the soul of *Spaine* to infuse designes into.

The Princes of *Italy* carefull to bind one another by common caution; restrained from the freedom of their own counsells, by force of stronger powers above them, and as busie keeping down their people, to multiply profit out of them, as to entise the stranger thither, to gain moderately by him. Through which narrow kind of wisdom, they being become rather Merchant than Monarchall States, were confined from challenging their own, or enlarging their dominions upon neighbors; and lastly, in aspect to other Princes rights, conjured within neutrall Circles, by the mysticall practise of an abusing
*Conclave*,

*Conclave*, and afpiring Monarch of *Spain*.

The *Mofcovite* bridled by his barbarous neighbor the *Tartar*; and through natural ignorance, and incivility, like a poor Tenant upon a rich Farm, unequall to his inferiors.

The *Grand Signior* afleep in his *Saraglia*; as having turned the ambition of that growing Monarchy into idle luft; corrupted his Martiall difcipline; prophaned his *Alcoran*, in making war againft his own Church, and not in perfon, but by his *Bafha's*; confequently by all apparance, declining into his people by fuch, but more precipitate degrees, as his active Anceftors had climbed above them.

Now while all thefe Princes lived thus fettered within the narrownefs of their own Eftates, or humors; *Spain* managing the *Popedome* by voices, and penfions among the Cardinals, and having the fword both by land, & fea in his hand; feemed likewife to have all thofe Weftern-parts of the world, laid as a *Tabula rafa* before him, to write
where

where he pleafed; *Yo el Ṛé*. And that which made this fatal profpect the more probable, was his golden Indian Mines; kept open, not only to feed, and carry his threatning Fleets, & Armies, where he had will, or right to goe; but to make way, and pretenfe for more, where he lift, by corrupting, and terrifying the chief Counfels both of Chriftian and Heathen Princes. Which tempting, and undermining courfe had already given fuch reputation both to his Civill and Martiall actions; that he was even then grown as impoffible to pleafe, as dangerous to offend.

Out of which fearfull Almanack this wakeful-Patriot, befides an univerfall terror upon all Princes, faw (as I faid) that this immenfe power of *Spain* did caft a more particular afpect of danger upon his native Countrey: and fuch as was not likely to be prevented, or fecured by any other Antidote, than a generall league among free Princes, to undertake this undertaker at home. To make this courfe plaufible, though he knew the Qu. of *England* had already
engaged

engaged her fortunes into it, by protecting the States Generall, yet perceiving her Governours (as I faid) to fit at home in their foft chairs, playing faft or loofe with them that ventured their lives abroad; he providently determined that while *Spain* had peace, a Pope, money, or credit; and the world men, neceffity, or humors; the war could hardly be determined upon this Low-Countrey ftage.

Becaufe if the neighbour-hood of *Flanders*, with help of the fuddain fea paffage, fhould tempt thefe united Princes to fall upon that limb of the *Spanifh* Empire; it would prove (as he fuppofed) an affailing of him in the ftrongeft feat of his war; where all exchanges, paffages, and fupplies were already fetled to his beft advantage: and fo a force bent againft him, even where himfelf could wifh it.

*Flanders* being a Province replenifhed with offenfive, and defenfive Armies: and fortified with divers ftrong Cities: of which the affailing Armies muft be conftrained, either to leave many behind them,

them, or elfe to hazard the lofs of time, and their gallanteft Troops in befieging of one.

Again he conceived that *France* it felf was like enough to be tender, in feconding our defignes with horfe, or foot there; our neighbour-hood upon the fame Continent (out of old acquaintance) not being over-welcome to them, as he prefumed. And for fuccors from other Princes; they were to come far, and pafs through divers dominions with difficulty, diftraction, lofs of time, and perchance loofe-handed difcipline.

And fo concludes, firft, that it would be hard for us to become abfolute Mafters of the field in *Flanders*, or to ground our affailing of him there upon any other argument, than that ever-betraying *Fallax* of undervaluing our enemies, or fetling undertaking Counfels upon market-mens Intelligence, as *Cæfar* faith the *French* in his time ufed to do. Which confident wayes, without any curious examination what power the adverfe party hath prepared to encounter, by defenfe, invafion, or divifion, muft
probably

probably make us losers, both in men, money, and reputation. And upon these and the like assumpsits he resolved there were but two ways left to frustrate this ambitious Monarchs designes. The one, that which diverted *Hanibal*, and by setting fire on his own house made him draw in his Spirits to comfort his heart; the other that of *Iason* by fetching away his golden Fleece, and not suffering any one man quietly to enjoy that, which every man so much affected.

## CHAP. IX.

TO carry war into the bowels of *Spain*, and by the assistance of the *Netherlands*, burn his shipping in all havens as they passed along; and in that passage surprize some well-chosen place for wealth, & strength: easie to be taken, and possible to be kept by us: he supposed to be the safest, most quick, and honourable Counsell of diversion. Because the same strength of shipping

shipping which was offensively imployed to carry forces thither; and by the way to interrupt all Martiall preparations, and provisions of that griping state; might by the convenient distance between his Coast, & ours (if the *Spaniard* should affect to pay us with our own monies) fitly be disposed both wayes; and so like two arms of a naturall body (with little addition of charge) defend, and offend; spend and supply at one time.

Or, if we found our own stock, or neighbours contribution strong enough to follow good success to greater designes; then whether our adventure once more, in stirring up spirit in the *Portugall* against the *Castilians* tyranny over them, were not to cast a chance for the best part of his wealth, reputation, & strength, both of men and shipping in all his dominions.

Again, left the pride of *Spain* should be secretly ordain'd to scourge it self, for having been a scourge to so many, and yet in this reall inquisition escape the audacity of undertaking Princes;

Sir *Philip* thought fit to put the world in mind, that *Sevill* was a fair City; secure in a rich soyl, and plentiful traffique; but an effeminate kind of people, guardded with a conquering name; and consequently a fair bait to the piercing eyes of ambitious Generals, needy Souldiers, and greedy Mariners. In like sort hee mentioned *Cales*, as a strength, and key to her traffiquefull, & navigable river, not fit to be neglected in such a defensive, and diverting enterprise, but at least to be examined.

Lastly, whether this audacity of undertaking the conqueror at home, would not, with any moderate success, raise up a new face of things in those parts; and suddainly stir up many spirits, to move against the same power, under which they long have bin slavishly conjur'd, & by this affront, prove a deforming blemish in the nice fortune of a fearfull usurper?

Or if that shall be thought an undertaking too full of charge, hazard, or difficulty; then whether it wil not be just in the wisdome of Estate, managed among

among active Princes; that as Qu. *Eliza-beth* had ever been tender, in preferving her Soveraignty upon the narrow feas; and wifely confidered, how nature, to maintain that birth-right of hers, had made all wars by fea far more cheap, proper, and commodious to her, than any expedition upon land could poffibly be : I fay, whether to continue this claim, would not prove honour to her felf, advantage to her traffique, and reputation to her people; I mean, if fhee fhould pleafe, in thofe cloudy humors, & queftions reigning between her felf, and other Princes, to keep a strong succeffive fleet, all feafonable times of the year, upon this pretty *Sleeve*, or *Ocean* of hers? I fay, to keep them as provident furveyers what did paffe from one ftate to another, wherein the law of Nature, or Nations had formerly given her intereft to an offenfive, or defenfive fecurity. A Regall inquifition, and worthy of a fea-Soveraign, without wronging friends, or neighbours, to have a perfect intelligence what they had, or wanted for delicacy, peace, or war in generall : And in particular

ticular, a clear perspective glass into her enemies Merchant, or Martiall traffique, enabling this Queen so to ballance this ambitious *Leviathan* in either kind; as the little fishes, his fellow Citizens, might travell, multiply, & live quietly by him under the protection of nature.

Again, let us consider, whether out of this, or the like Audit, it will not be found a just tribute to opportunity, the rudder of all state wisedoms. That as Qu. *Elizabeth* was a Soveraign, which rested with her sex at home, and yet moved all sexes abroad to their own good; whether (I say) as she from a devoted zeal to the Church, had by Sir *Nich. Throgmorton*, in the beginning of her reign, stirred up spirits in that over-mitred *French* Kingdom, to become watchful guardians of peace, and Religion there. I say, whether in the same Christian providence there might not, by the neglect, or breach of many Treaties, an occasion be justly taken to reap a reasonable harvest out of that well-chosen seed time, by receiving *Rochel*, *Brest*, *Bourdeaux*, or any other place

place upon that Continent, diſtreſſed for Religion, into her abſolute protection? Neverthelefs, not with intent of reconquering any part of her ancient Domaines, lineally defcended from many anceſtors; howſoever thofe places fo taken may feem feated like tempters of Princes, to plead in the Court of *Mars* fuch native, though difcontinued rights, as no time can prefcribe againſt; but only to keep thofe humble religious fouls from oppreſſion, in that fuper-Jefuited foveraignty.

In which religious defigne to encourage the Qu. he adviſed us to examine if the diviſions naturally rifing amongſt their unlimited *French Grandees*, grown up *per faltum* with their Kings above Laws, Parliaments, and Peoples freedom; would not in all probability caſt up fom light duſt into their fuperiors eys, as tributes to their common Idol *Diſorder*; and fo perchance either by treaty, or fight of the firſt Army, ſtir up *Bouillon*, & *Rohan* for Religion; other Roytelets w[th] hope to make fafe their fubaltern governments, even through the

the ruines of that over-foaring foveraignty?

And is it not as probable again, that even the greateft Cities, raifed and ftanding upon the like waving encroachments of time, & advantagious power would readily become jealous of the leaft ftrict hand carried over them, by interruption of traffique, greedinefs of Governors, pride of their own wealth, or indefinite impofitions; as *Paris*, *Bourdeaux*, *Marfeilles*, *Roan*, or *Lyons*? whereby they might likewife be tempted, either to run head-long with the ftream, or at the leaft to ftand at gaze, and leave the Heraldry of Princes to be decided by the ftronger party, as for the most part, they hitherto have been.

Nay in this Climax to come nearer yet; is it probable that even the Catholique Princes, and Provinces environing this vaft Kingdome, would (as now they doe) for want of vent, break their hopes, and fervilly run out upon the ground like water, and not rather when this new rent fhould appear, chufe to fhake off a chargeable, & fervile yoke of
Mountebank

Mountebank holinefs under *Spanish Rome*, and to that end prefently mingle money, councels, and forces with ours? As quickly refolved that this way of a ballancing union, amongft abfolute Princes, would prove quieter reft for them, and founder foundations for us than our former parties did, when we conquered *France*, more by fuch factious & ambitious affiftances, than by any odds of our Bows, or Beef-eaters, as the *French* were then fcornfully pleas'd to terme us: I fay, even when in the pride of our conquefts, we ftrove to gripe more than was poffible for us to hold: as appears by our being forced to come away, and leave our anceftors bloud, and bones behind, for Monuments not of enjoying, but of over-griping & expulfion.

So that the fum of all is; whether the taking or furprize of *Calice, Rochel, Bourdeaux*, or fome fuch other good out, or inlet upon that Mayn, offered into our protection, would not prove honour to us, as a brave earneft either to war, or peace? Beneficiall to the *French* King, and

and Crown againſt their wills ; as mani-feſting to their hot ſpirits, and young Councels, that undertaking is not all? And beſides clearly ſhewing, in *Mars* his true glaſs, how that once wel-formed Monarchy had by little, and little, let fal her ancient, and reverend pillars, (I mean Parliaments, Lawes, and Cuſtomes) into the narrowneſs of Proclamations, or Imperiall Mandates : by which like baſtard children of tyranny ſhe hath transformed her Gentry into Peaſants, her Peaſants into ſlaves, Magiſtracy into Sale works, Crown-revenue into Impoſitions. And therein likewiſe publiſhed the differences between Monarchs, and Tyrants ſo clearly to the world, as here-after all Eſtates, that would take upon their necks the yoke of Tyranny, muſt juſtly be reputed voluntary ſlaves in the choice of that paſſive bondage.

Whereby, one queſtion naturally be-getting another, the next (as I take it) muſt be what this Auſtrian aſpiring familie would doe, while theſe two Kingdoms ſhould ſtand thus engaged? Whether invade the King of *Denmark* alone,

alone, hoping by his ruine to fubdue the yet unfubdued Princes of *Germany*; to get the Sound, and Eaftern Seas, with all their Maritime riches into his power: to bring the Hanfe Towns into fome captivated fubjections, and thereby become Soveraign over all *Eaftern* traffique by Sea, and land? Or elfe by lulling *France* afleep with Imperiall Matches, or promifes, finde means to fteal the Flower-de-luce into the Lyons garland; and in that currant of profperity to Citadellize the long oppreffed *Netherlands* into a tenure of uttermoft bondage; and fo build up his Eagles neft above the threatning of any inferior Region.

But it many times pleafeth God by the breaking out of concealed flafhes from thefe fatall cloudes of craft, or violence, to awake even the moft fuperftitious Princes out of their enchanted dreams; and caufe them to refolve fuddainly to make head againft this devouring *Sultan*, with leagues offenfive, and defenfive. And by an unexpected union to become fuch frontier neighbours to this Crown-hunter, as he might with great reafon

reafon doubt their treading upon his large cloven feet, who intended to have fet them fo heavily upon the heads of many more ancient States, Peoples, or Scepters than his own. And laftly, in the fame prefs, by this one affront in the Lions face, publifhing to the world that power is infinite no where but in God : fo as the firft blow well ftricken, moft commonly fucceeds with honor, and advantage to the judicious, able, and active undertakers.

Out of which divine providence, governing all fecond caufes by the firft; is it not probable that even the naturall viciffitudes of war, and peace, would bring forth fome active propofitions between thefe many waies allied Kingdomes of *England*, and *France*, to a perfect reconciliation, and as many again of irreconciliable divifion between them, and *Spain*? *France* being ftirred up by a joint counfell, and propofition of affiftance, to the recovery of her long fleeping rights in *Navarre*, or *Naples*; and *England* onely to diftract this ambitious Monarch from his late Cuftom,

in

in depofing Kings, and Princes as *Navarre*, *Portugall*, the *Palatine*, *Brunfwick*, &c., and as in a fecond courfe of his devouring gluttony, interrupt him from future profecutions of *Denmark*, and *Germany* it felf, to the fame end; with this conftant intent, to bring all the earth under one mans tyranny.

To prevent which deluge of boundlefs power, Sir *Philip* was of opinion, that more than charge, it could be no prejudice; if to the unvizarding of this masked triplicity between *Spain*, *Rome* and the Soveraign Iefuits of *France*; I fay if the *Queen*, as defendrefs of the faith, for a main pledg of this new offenfive, and defenfive undertaken league, would be pleafed to affift the French King with the fame forces by Sea, or land, wherewith, till then, fhe had juftly oppofed againft him. And confequently putting the Spaniard from an offenfive, to a defenfive War, manifeftly publifh, and give credit to this unbelieved truth, *viz*. that this Arch-Conqueror never intended other favor to the Pope, Emperor, or Iefuits, in all this

this conjunction, than *Poliphemus* promised to *Ulysses*, which was, that they should be the last whom he purposed to devour.

And farther to encourage these great Princes in this true balancing designe with the chargeable, and thorny passages proper to it; he providently saw the long threatned Dutchie of *Savoy* would be in their view: with assurance that this active Prince would think it a safe diversion of dangers from his domesticall Estate, and a fit stage to act his forrain cobwebbs upon, if he might have them shadowed under the wings of stronger, and every way more able Powers; without which his mean Estate must in all probability force him to shift his outward garments perchance too often.

The *Venetians* again, foreseeing with their Aristocraticall jealousie, that their Estate had onely two pregnant dangers hanging over it; the one Eastward from the grand Signior, who easily moves not his encompassing half Moon; the other Westward from this *Solyman* of *Spain*, whose unsatiable ambition, they knew, would

would reft upon no centre, but creep along the Mediterranean Seas, till he might (contrary to the nature of thofe waters) over-flow all weak, or fecure neighbor Princes, without any other title, or quarrell, than *Stet pro ratione voluntas*. And forefeeing again in this fuddain violence, that they could expect no Eftate to be felfly engaged in their fuccor; but muft refolve to ftand, or fall alone by that courfe. Where, on the other fide, if the Eaftern half Moon fhould but feem to move towards them; they were affured to have all the Eftates of *Europe*, engaged by their own interefts, to joine with them. Upon this view there is no doubt, but that wife City would have refolved it to be a choice of lefs evill, to joine with thefe great Princes, in diverting his Spanifh gallies, and galleons by Sea, and his inveterate Armies by land from difturbing, or fubjecting the fafety, and traffique of all Chriftendom to his feven patch'd coated Kingdomes, rather than for want of heart or opportunity, to ftand neuter (as they doe) and become
treafurers

treasurers both of money, and munition for him, that already intends thus to conquer them, and enjoy it.

Again, shall we (said Sir *Philip*) in these collections of particulars, forget the state of *Italy* it self? which excellent temper of spirits, earth, and aire, having long been smothered, and mowed down by the differing Tyrannies of *Spain*, and *Rome*, shall we not be confident they would, upon the approaching of these armies, both stir up those benumbed Soveraignties, which onely bear the name of free Princes, to affect their own Manumissions, & help to chase away those succeeding and oppressing Garrisons, whose fore-fathers for many yeares had sold life, libertie, and lawes for eight pence the day; and so resolutely oppose those Spanish-born, or Spanish-sworn Tyrannies, which have for divers ages Lorded over that most equally tempered Nation?

Or whether the winter in those Seas, giving opportunity without suspition, may not encourage the Claim of our old rights in the Kingdom of *Sicilie*,

more

more legall than moſt of his Spaniſh intruſions; and therein be welcome to the Grand Signior, the freedom of *Algiers*, even to *Italy* it ſelf. And beſides, if we proſpered, yield abundance of wealth by ſpoil, and trade: with ſuch a ſeat for diverſion, or poſſeſſion, as by many viſible, and inviſible helps, might be kept, or put away with infinite advantage?

Laſtly, he made a Quære, whether the Pope himſelf would not (like a ſecular Prophet) to keep his becoming Chaplain a little the farther off; either wink, or at leaſt delay his thundering curſes, or ſupplies of *Peter-pence* againſt theſe qualifying Armies, onely to moderate the over-greatneſſe of this Spaniſh Monarchie? whoſe infancie having been nouriſhed under the Miters holy water, and ſophiſtries of his practiſing *Conclaves*, dares now imperiouſly publiſh to the world a reſolution, of taking all other diſtinctions from amongſt men, ſaving that Canonicall regiment of wit and might, whereby he might ſo preſerve his ſpirituall ambition

bition entire, without any charge or change of Religion, or Soveraignties from one hand to another, but like a holy father mediate the reftoring of *Italy* to her ancient free, and diftinct Principalities. Whereby now by this moderate courfe, admit the Pope for his part, fhould impair his temporall profits, and fubaltern jurisdiction a while; yet fhall he be fure, (as I faid) to multiply his fpirituall honors, and inlarge that Kingdom, by thefe works of *Supererogation.* And by joyning with his fellow Princes in a contribution, by way of accompt, or countenance to pay thefe great Armies, be fure to fit rent-free under his, and their own vines, as abfolute fpirituall, and temporall Princes ought to doe?

From which (faith he) this conclufion will probably follow; that the undertaking of this *Antonie* fingle, I mean *France*, would prove a begetting of brave occafions jointly to difturb this Spanifh *Ottoman*, in all his waies of crafty, or forcible conquefts. Efpecially fince *Queen Elizabeth*, the ftandard of this

this conjunction, would infallibly incline to unite with the better part, and by a fuddain changing of *Mars* his Imperious Enfignes, into a well ballanced treaty of univerfall Peace, reftore and keep the world within her old *equilibrium* or bounds.

And the rather, becaufe her long cuftom in governing, would quickly have made her difcern, that it had been impoffible, by force, or any human wifdom to have qualified thofe over-grown Combinations of *Spain*; but onely by a countermining of party with party, and a diftracting of exorbitant defires, by cafting a gray-headed cloud of fear over them; thereby manifefting the well difguifed yokes of bondage, under which our Modern Conquerors would craftily entice the Nown-adjective-natured Princes, and fubjects of this time to fubmit their necks. A map (as it pleafed her to fay) of his fecrets, in which fhe confeffed herfelf to be the more ripe, because under the like falfe Enfignes, though perchance better mafked, fhe had feen *Philip* the fecond after the fame meafure, measure, or with little difference, to *Henry* the third of *France*, a principall fellow-member in that earthly founded, though heavenly seeming Church of *Rome*, when he redelivered *Amiens*, *Abbeville*, &c. together with that souldier-like passage made by the Duke of *Parma* through *France*, to the relief of *Paris*. Yet whether this provident *Philip* did frame these specious charities of a conqueror, *Augustus*-like, aspiring to live after death greater than his successor; or providently foreseeing that the divers humors in succeeding Princes, would prove unable to maintain such green usurpations, in the heart of a Kingdom competitor with his seven-headed *Hydra* kept together onely by a constant and unnaturall wheel of fortune, till some new child of hers, like *Henry* the fourth, should take his turn in restoring all unjust combinations or encrochments; or lastly, whether, like a true cutter of Cumine seedes, he did not craftily lay these hypocritall sacrifices upon the Altar of death, as peace-offerings from pride to the temple of fear, or smoaks of of a dying difeafed confcience choked up with innocent bloud: of all which perplexed pedigrees, I know not what to determine otherwife; than that thefe Tyrannicall encrochments doe carry the images of Hell, and her thunder-workers, in their own breafts, as fortune doth misfortunes in that wind-blown, vaft, and various womb of hers.

Or if this fhould feem of too high a nature, or too many chargeable parts: then whether to begin again where we left, and by the example of *Drake*, a mean born fubject to the Crown of *England*, invade, poffefs, & inhabite fome well chofen havens in *Peru*, *Mexico*, or both, were not to ftrike at the root, & affail him where he is weakeft; & yet gathers his chiefeft ftrength to make himfelf Monarch over all the Weftern Climes? fupplyes being as eafie to us, as to him, we having both winds, and feas indifferently open between us.

*CHAP.*

## CHAP. X.

UPon due confideration of which particulars, he fore-feeing that each of the former required greater refolution, union, and expenfe, than the neutrality, diffidence, and quiet complexion of the Princes then reigning could well bear; and befides the freedome of choyce to bee taken away, or at the leaft obftructed by fatall mifts of ignorance, or factious counfells reigning among the Minifters of Kings: he refolved from the grounds of his former intended voiage with Sir *Francis Drake*, that the only credible means left, was, to affail him by invafion, or incurfion (as occafion fell out) in fome part of that rich, and defert Weft-Indian Man.

Firft, becaufe it is an obfervation among the wifeft, that as no man is a Prophet in his own Countrey; fo all men may get honour much cheaper far off

off than at home, and at fea more eafily than at land.

Secondly, in refpect he difcovered the Spanifh conquefts in thofe remote parts, fo much noifed throughout the world, to be indeed like their Jefuits Miracles; which comming far, were multiplied by Fame and Art, to keep other Nations in wonder, and blind worfhip.

Thirdly, out of confident beliefe, that their inhumane cruelties had fo difpeopled, & difpleafed thofe countreys; that as he was fure to find no great power to withftand him; fo might he well hope the Reliques of thofe oppreffed *Cimerons* would joyfully take Arms with any forrainer to redeem their liberty, and revenge their parents bloud.

Fourthly, by reafon the fcale of diftance between *Spain* & *America* was fo great; as it infallibly affured Sir *Philip*, he fhould find leafure enough to land, fortifie, and become Mafter of the field, before any fuccour could come thither to interrupt him.

Fiftly,

Fiftly, the pride, delicacy, and security of the *Spaniard*, which made him live without Difcipline; and trust more to the greatnefs of his name abroad, than any ftrength, order, courage, or munition at home.

Sixtly, Sir *Philip* prophecying what the pedigrees of Princes did warrant, I mean the happy conjunction of *Scotland*, to thefe populous Realms of *England* & *Ireland*; forefaw, that if this multitude of people were not ftudioufly husbanded, and difpofed, they would rather diminifh, than add any ftrength to this Monarchy. Which danger (he conjectured) could only by this defigne of forrain imploiment, or the peaceable harvest of manufactures at home, be fafely prevented.

The feventh, and a chief motive indeed was, that no other action could be lefs fubject to emulation of Court, lefs ftraining to the prefent humors of State, more concurring with expectation, and voice of time; nor wherein there was greater poffibility of improving merit, wealth, & friends.

Laftly,

Lastly, he did, as all undertakers must doe, believe that there is ever good intelligence between chance & hazard, and so left some things not summed up before hand by exact minutes. But rather thought good to venture upon the cast of a *Rubicon* Dy; either to stop his springs of gold, and so drie up that torrent which carried his subduing Armies every where; or else by the wakefull providence of threatned neighbors, force him to waft home that conquering Metall with infinite charge, and notwithstanding unwarranted from enriching those enemies, whom he principally studied to supprefs by it.

To confirm which opinion, he foresaw how this over-racked unity of the *Spanish* government (intending to work a change in the free course of nature) had interdicted all manufacture, traffick, or vent by sea, or land, between the natives of *America*, & all nations else, *Spain* excepted. And withall, to make the barrenness of *Spain* more fertile, how he had improved that idle *Castilian*, by imployments, in activeness, wealth, and authority

authority over thofe vanquifhed creatures; fuffering the poor native *Americans* to be fuppreft with heavy impofitions, difcouraging idlenefs, bondage of laws, fheering of the humble fheep to cloath the proud devouring Wolves; finally, under thefe, & fuch like quinteffences of tyranny ftriving (as I faid) even befides nature, to make barren *Spain* the Monarchy, & that every way more fertile *America* to be the Province. All which affectations of power to be wifer, & ftronger than the truth, this Gentleman concluded would in fulnes of time make manifeft; that the heavy can no more be forced to afcend, and reft fixed there, than the light to goe downward, as to their proper center.

 Notwithftanding, the ftate of Tyrants is fo fublime, and their errors founded upon fuch precipitate fteps, as this growing *Spaniard* both did, doth, and ever will travell (with his forefathers in Paradife) to be equall, or above his Maker; and fo to imprifon divine laws within the narrownes of will, and humane wifdome, with the fettred felfneffes

neſſes of cowardly or over-confident Tyranny. In which prepoſterous courſes, to prevent all poſſibility of commotion, let the Reader be pleaſed to obſerve, how that continually he forceth his own ſubjects free-denized in *America*, to fetch weapons of defence, conqueſt, invaſion; as well as ornament, wealth, neceſſity, and delicacy, out of *Spain*, meerly to retain want, ſupply, price, weight, faſhion, and meaſure, ſtill (contrary to nature) in that barren Crown of *Caſtile*, with an abſolute power reſting in himſelf to rack, or eaſe both peoples, according to the waving ends of an unſteddy, and ſharp pointed Pyramis of power.

Nay, to riſe yet a ſtep higher in this bloudy pride; Sir *Philip*, our unbelieved *Caſſandra*, obſerved this limitleſs ambition of the *Spaniard* to have choſen that uttermoſt Citadell of bondage, I mean the Inquiſition of *Spain*, for her inſtrument. Not, as in former Maſks, to prune, or govern; but in a confidence riſing out of the old age of ſuperſtitious fantaſms, utterly to root out all ſeeds of of humane freedom; and (as Sr *Philip* conceived) with fatal diffolution to it felf. In refpect that thefe types of extremity would foon publifh to the world, what little difference Tyrants ftrive to leave between the creation, ufe, and honor of men, and beafts, valuing them indifferently but as Counters, to fum up the divers, nay contrary ufes, and Audits of fublime and wandring fupremacy, which true glafs would (in this Gentlemans opinion) fhew the moft dull & cowardly eye, that Tyrants be not nurfing Fathers, but ftep-fathers; and fo no anointed deputies of God, but rather lively Images of the dark Prince, that fole author of dif-creation, and diforder, who ever ruines his ends with over-building.

Laftly, where his reafon ended, there many divine Precepts, and Examples did affure him, that the vengeance of God muft neceffarily hang over thofe hypocriticall cruelties, which under colour of converting fouls to him, fent millions of better than their own, they cared not whither: And in ftead of
fpreading

spreading Christian religion by good life, committed such terrible inhumanities, as gave those that lived under nature manifest occasion to abhor the devily characters of so tyrannical a deity.

Now though this justice of the Almighty be many times slow, & therefore neglected here on earth; yet (I say) under the only conduct of this star did Sir *Philip* intend to revive this hazardous enterprize of Planting upon the Main of *America*; projected, nay undertaken long before, (as I shewed you) but ill executed in the absence of Sir *Philip*; with a designe to possess *Nombre de Dios*, or some other haven near unto it, as places, in respect of the little distance between the two seas, esteemed the fittest *Rendez-vouz* for supply, or retreat of an Army upon all occasions. And besides, by that means to circle in his wealth and freedome, with a joynt fore-running Fleet; to the end, that if the fortune of Conquest prospered not with them, yet he should infallibly pay the charge of both Navies,

Navies, with infinite lofs, and dif-reputation to the *Spaniard*.

And in this project Sir *Philip* proceeded fo far with the united Provinces, as they yeelded to affift, and fecond the fhips of his Soveraign, under his charge, with a fleet of their own. Which, befides a prefent addition of ftrength, he knew would lead in others by example.

Again, for fupply of thefe Armies, he had (out of that naturall tribute, which all free fpirits acknowledge to fuperior worth) won 30 Gentlemen of great bloud, and ftate here in *England*, every man to fell one hundred pounds land, to fecond, and countenance this firft Fleet with a ftronger.

Now when thefe beginnings were by his own credit and induftrie thus well fetled: then to give an excellent form to a reall work, hee contrived this new intended Plantation, not like an *Affylum* for fugitives, a *Bellum Piraticum* for *Banditi*, or any fuch bafe *Ramas* of people; but as an *Emporium* for the confluence of all Nations that love, or profefs

profefs any kinde of vertue, or Commerce.

Wherein to incite thofe that tarried at home to adventure, he propounded the hope of a fure, and rich return. To Martiall men he opened wide the door of fea and land, for fame and conqueft. To the nobly ambitious the far ftage of *America*, to win honour in. To the Religious divines, befides a new Apoftolicall calling of the laft heathen to the Chriftian faith, a large field of reducing poor Chriftians, mif-led by the Idolatry of *Rome*, to their mother *Primitive* Church. To the ingenuoufly induftrious, variety of natural richeffes, for new myfteries, and manufactures to work upon. To the Merchant, with a fimple people, a fertile, and unexhaufted earth. To the fortune-bound, liberty. To the curious, a fruitfull womb of innovation. Generally the word gold was an attractive Adamant, to make men venture that which they have, in hope to grow rich by that which they have not.

What the expectation of this voyage was,

was, the time paſt can beſt witnes; but what the ſucceſs ſhould have been (till it be revived by ſome ſuch generous undertaker) lies hid in Gods ſecret judgements, who did at once cut off this Gentlemans life, and ſo much of our hope.

Upon theſe enterpriſes of his, I have preſumed to ſtand the longer, becauſe from the aſhes of this firſt propounded voyage to *America*, that fatall *Low Country* action ſprang up, in which this worthy Gentleman loſt his life. Beſides, I do ingenuouſly confeſs, that it delights me to keep company with him, even after death; eſteeming his actions, words, and converſation, the daintieſt treaſure my mind could then lay up; or can at this day impart with our poſteritie.

## CHAP. XI.

THerefore to come at the laſt to that diverting imployment, promiſed to him under his Uncle in the Low-Countries: he was, upon his return

return to the Court, inftantly made for Garrifon, Governor of *Flufhing*, and for the Field, General of the Horfe; in both which charges, his carriage teftified to the world, wifdome, and valour, with addition of honour to his Country by them.

For inftance; how like a Souldier did he behave himfelf, firft in contriving, then in executing the furprife of *Axil?* where he revived that ancient, and fecure difcipline of order, & filence in their March; and after their entrance into the town, placed a band of choice fouldiers to make a ftand in the Marketplace, for fecuritie to the reft, that were forced to wander up and down by direction of Commanders; and when the fervice was done, rewarded that obedience of difcipline in every one, liberally, out of his own purfe.

How providently again did he preferve the lives and honor of our Englifh Army, at that enterprife of *Gravelin?* where though he was guided by directions given him; yet whether out of arguments drawn from the perfon of

*La*

*La Motte*, Commander of that town, who had a generall reputation of too much worth, either *Sinon*-like to deceive, or eafily to be deceived; or out of the ftrength and importance of that place, precious to the owner in many refpects, the leaft of which would redouble lofs to the growing ambition of a Conqueror; or whether upon caution given by intelligence; or whatfoever light of diverfion elfe; he (I fay) was refolute not to hazzard fo many principall Gentlemen, with fuch gallant Troops and Commanders which accompanied him, in that flattering expedition. Yet becaufe he kept this fteady counfel in his own bofome, there was labouring on every fide to obtain the honour of that fervice. To all which gallant kind of competition, he made this anfwer, that his own comming thither was to the fame end, wherein they were now become his rivalls; & therfore affured them, that he would not yeeld any thing to any man, which by right of his place was both due to himfelf, and confequently difgrace for him to execute
by

by others: again, that by the fame rule, he would never confent to hazzard them that were his friends, and in divers refpects his equalls, where he found reafon to make many doubts, and fo little reafon to venture himfelf.

Yet as a Commander, concluding fomething fit to be done, equally for obedience and triall, he made the inferior fort of Captains try their fortune by dice upon a drums head: the lot fell upon Sir *William Brown* his own Lieutenant, who with a choice company prefently departed, receiving this provifionall caution from Sir *Philip*, that if he found practife, & not faith, he fhould ftreight throw down his Arms, and yeeld himfelf prifoner; protefting that if they took him, he fhould be ranfomed; if they broke quarter, his death moft feverely revenged.

On thefe forlorn companies go with this Leader, & before they came into the town, found all outward fignals exactly performed; when they were entred, every ftreet fafe and quiet, according to promife, till they were
paft

past any easie recovery of the gate; then instantly out of the cellars under ground, they were charged by Horse and Foot. The Leader, following his Generalls commandement, discovers the treason, throws down his arms, and is taken prisoner. The rest of the company retire, or rather fly towards their ships, but stil wounded and cut off by pursuit of their enemies; till at length a Serjeant of a band, with fifteen more, all *Sidney*'s men (I mean such as could die to win honour, and do service to their country) made a halt, and being fortunately mixt of pikes, halberds, and muskets, resolved to be slain with their backs to their friends, and their faces to their enemies; they moved, or staied with occasion; and were in both continually charged with Foot and Horse, till in the end eight were slain, and eight left alive. With these the Serjeant wounded in the side with a square die out of a field-piece, made this brave retreat within view, and at last protection of their own Navy; bringing home even in the wounds, nay
ruins

ruins of himfelf, and company, reputation of courage, and Martiall difcipline to his Country.

Moreover, in thofe private accidents of difcontentment & quarrell, which naturally accompany great fpirits in the beft governed Camps, how difcreetly did Sir *Philip* ballance that brave *Hollock*, made head of a party againft his Uncle? When putting himfelf between indignities offered to his Soveraign, through the Earl of *Leicefters* perfon; and yet not fit for a fupreme Governors place to ground a duel upon; he brought thofe paffionate charges, which the Count *Hollock* addreffed upwards to the Earl, down by degrees upon himfelf. Where that brave Count *Hollock* found Sir *Philip* fo fortified with wifdom, courage, and truth; befides the ftrong partie of former friendfhip ftanding for him in the Counts noble nature; as though fenfe of honour, and many things elfe equal, and unequal between them, were in apparance beyond poffibilitie of peecing; yet this one inequality of right on Sir *Philip*'s fide, made the propounder calm;

calm; and by coming to terms of expoſtulation, did not only reconcile thoſe two worthy ſpirits, one to another, more firmly than before; but withall through himſelf wrought, if not a kind of unitie between the Earl of *Leiceſter*, and the Count *Hollock*, at leaſt a finall ſurceaſe of all violent jealouſies, or factious expoſtulations.

Theſe particulars I only point out, leaving the reſt for them, that may, perchance, write larger ſtories of that time. To be ſhort; not in complements and art, but reall proofe given of his ſufficience above others, in very little time his reputation, and authority amongſt that active people grew ſo faſt, as it had been no hard matter for him, with the diſadvantage of his Uncle, and diſtraction of our affairs in thoſe parts, to have raiſed himſelf a fortune there. But in the whole courſe of his life, he did ſo conſtantly ballance ambition with the ſafe precepts of divine, and moral duty, as no pretence whatſoever could have entiſed that Gentleman, to break through the circle of a good Patriot.

*CHAP.*

## CHAP. XII.

THus fhall it fuffice me to have trod out fome fteps of this *Britane Scipio*, thereby to give the learned a fcantling, for drawing out the reft of his dimenfions by proportion. And to the end the abruptnefs of this Treatife may fuit more equally with his fortune, I will cut off his Actions, as God did his Life, in the midft; and fo conclude with his death.

In which paffage, though the pride of flefh, and glory of Mankind be commonly fo allayed, as the beholders feldome fee any thing elfe in it, but objects of horror, and pittie; yet had the fall of this man fuch natural degrees, that the wound whereof he died, made rather an addition, than diminution to his fpirits. So that he fhewed the world, in a fhort progrefs to a long home, paffing fair, and wel-drawn lines; by the guide of which, all pilgrims of this life may conduct

duct themselves humbly into the haven of everlasting rest.

When that unfortunate stand was to be made before *Zutphen*, to stop the issuing out of the Spanish Army from a streict; with what alacrity soever he went to actions of honor, yet remembring that upon just grounds the ancient Sages describe the worthiest persons to be ever best armed, he had compleatly put on his; but meeting the Marshall of the Camp lightly armed (whose honour in that art would not suffer this unenvious *Themistocles* to sleep) the unspotted emulation of his heart, to venture without any inequalitie, made him cast off his Cuisses; and so, by the secret influence of destinie, to disarm that part, where God (it seems) had resolved to strike him. Thus they go on, every man in the head of his own Troop; and the weather being misty, fell unawares upon the enemie, who had made a strong stand to receive them, near to the very walls of *Zutphen*; by reason of which accident their Troops fell, not only unexpectedly to be engaged within the levell of the
great

great shot, that played from the Rampiers, but more fatally within shot of their Muskets, which were layd in ambush within their own trenches.

Now whether this were a desperate cure in our Leaders, for a desperate disease; or whether misprision, neglect, audacity, or what else induced it, it is no part of my office to determine, but onely to make the narration clear, and deliver rumor, as it passed then, without any stain, or enammel.

Howsoever, by this stand, an unfortunate hand out of those forespoken Trenches, brake the bone of Sir *Philip's* thigh with a Musket-shot. The horse he rode upon, was rather furiously cholleric, than bravely proud, and so forced him to forsake the field, but not his back, as the noblest, and fittest biere to carry a Martiall Commander to his grave. In which sad progress, passing along by the rest of the Army, where his Uncle the Generall was, and being thirstie with excess of bleeding, he called for drink, which was presently brought him; but as he was putting the bottle to his mouth, he faw a poor Souldier carryed along, who had eaten his laft at the fame Feaft, gaftly cafting up his eyes at the bottle. Which Sir *Philip* perceiving, took it from his head, before he drank, and delivered it to the poor man, with thefe words, *Thy neceßity is yet greater than mine.* And when he had pledged this poor fouldier, he was prefently carried to *Arnheim*.

Where the principal Chirurgions of the Camp attended for him; fome mercinarily out of gain, others out of honour to their Art, but the moft of them with a true zeal (compounded of love and reverence) to doe him good, and (as they thought) many Nations in him. When they began to drefs his wound, he both by way of charge, and advice, told them, that while his ftrength was yet entire, his body free from feaver, and his mind able to endure, they might freely ufe their art, cut, and fearch to the bottome. For befides his hope of health, he would make this farther profit of the pains which he muft
suffer,

suffer, that they should bear witness, they had indeed a sensible natured man under their hands, yet one to whom a stronger Spirit had given power above himself, either to do, or suffer. But if they should now neglect their Art, and renew torments in the declination of nature, their ignorance, or over-tenderness would prove a kind of tyranny to their friend, and consequently a blemish to their reverend science.

With love and care well mixt, they began the cure, and continued it some sixteen dayes, not with hope, but rather such confidence of his recovery, as the joy of their hearts over-flowed their discretion, and made them spread the intelligence of it to the *Queen*, and all his noble friends here in *England*, where it was received, not as private, but publique good news.

Onely there was one Owle among all the birds, which though looking with no less zealous eyes than the rest, yet saw, and presaged more despair: I mean an excellent Chirurgion of the Count *Hollocks*, who although the Count himself lay at the same inftant hurt in the throat with a Mufket fhot, yet did he neglect his own extremitie to fave his friend, and to that end had fent him to Sir *Philip*. This Chirurgion notwithftanding (out of love to his Mafter) returning one day to drefs his wound, the Count cheerfully afked him how Sir *Philip* did? And being anfwered with a heavy countenance, that he was not well; at thefe words the worthy Prince (as having more fenfe of his friends wounds, than his own) cries out, Away villain, never fee my face again, till thou bring better news of that mans recovery; for whofe redemption many fuch as I were happily loft.

This honourable act I relate, to give the world one modern example; firft, that greatnefs of heart is not dead every where; and then, that war is both a fitter mould to fafhion it, and ftage to act it on, than peace can be; and laftly, that the reconciliation of enemies may prove fafe, and honourable, where the ciment on either fide
is

is worth. So as this *Florentine* precept concerning reconciled enemies, deferves worthily to be buried with unworthines the author of it, or at leaft the practife of it cryed down, and banifhed, to reign among barbarous heathen fpirits, who while they think life the uttermoft of all things, hold it fafe in no body that their own errors make doubtfull to them. And fuch feems every man that moves any paffion, but pleafure, in thofe intricate natures.

Now after the fixteenth day was paft, and the very fhoulder-bones of this delicate Patient worn through his skin, with conftant, and obedient pofturing of his body to their Art; he judicioufly obferving the pangs his wound ftang him with by fits, together with many other fymptoms of decay, few or none of recovery, began rather to fubmit his body to thefe Artifts, than any farther to believe in them. During which fufpenfe, he one morning lifting up the clothes for change & eafe of his body, fmelt fome extraordinary noifom favor about him, differing from oyls and

and salvs, as he conceived; & either out of naturall delicacy, or at least care not to offend others, grew a little troubled with it; which they that sate by perceiving, besought him to let them know what suddain indisposition he felt? Sir *Philip* ingenuously told it, and desired them as ingenuously to confess, whether they felt any such noisome thing, or no? They all protested against it upon their credits. Whence Sir *Philip* presently gave this severe doom upon himself; that it was inward mortification, and a welcome messenger of death.

Shortly after, when the Chirurgions came to dress him, he acquainted them with these piercing intelligences between him, and his mortality. Which though they opposed by authority of books, paralleling of accidents, and other artificiall probabilities; yet moved they no alteration in this man, who judged too truly of his own estate, and from more certain grounds, than the vanity of opinion in erring artificers could possibly pierce into. So that afterwards,

wards, how freely foever he left his body fubject to their practife, and continued a patient beyond exception; yet did he not change his minde, but as having caft off all hope, or defire of recovery, made, and divided that little fpan of life which was left him in this manner.

## CHAP. XIII.

First, he called the Minifters unto him; who were all excellent men, of divers Nations, and before them made fuch a confeffion of Chriftian faith, as no book but the heart can truly, and feelingly deliver. Then defired them to accompany him in Prayer, wherein hee befought leave to lead the affembly, in refpect, (as he faid) that the fecret fins of his own heart were beft known to himfelf, and out of that true fenfe, he more properly inftructed to apply the eternall Sacrifice of our Saviours Paffion and Merits to him.

His

His religious Zeal prevailed with this humbly devout, & afflicted company; In which wel chosen progress of his, howsoever they were all moved, and those sweet motions witnessed by sighes and tears, even interrupting their common devotion; yet could no man judge in himself, much less in others, whether this racke of heavenly agony, whereupon they all stood, were forced by sorrow for him, or admiration of him; the fire of this *Phenix* hardly being able out of any ashes to produce his equall, as they conceived.

Here this first mover stayed the motions in every man, by staying himself. Whether to give rest to that frail wounded flesh of his, unable to bear the bent of eternity so much affected, any longer; or whether to abstract that spirit more inwardly, and by chewing as it were the cudd of meditation, to imprint those excellent images in his soul; who can judge but God? Notwithstanding, in this change, (it should seem) there was little, or no change in the object. For instantly after prayer, he he entreated this quire of divine Philofophers about him, to deliver the opinion of the ancient Heathen, touching the immortality of the foul; Firft, to fee what true knowledge fhe retains of her own effence, out of the light of her felf; then to parallel with it the moft pregnant authorities of the old, and new Teftament, as fupernatural revelations, fealed up from our flefh, for the divine light of faith to reveal, and work by. Not that he wanted inftruction, or affurance; but becaufe this fixing of a lovers thoughts upon thofe eternall beauties, was not only a cheering up of his decaying fpirits, but as it were a taking poffeffion of that immortall inheritance, which was given unto him by his brother-hood in CHRIST.

The next change ufed, was the calling for his Will; which though at firft fight it may feem a defcent from heaven to earth again; yet he that obferves the diftinction of thofe offices, which he practifed in beftowing his own, fhall difcern, that as the foul of man is all in all, and all in every part; fo was the

the goodnes of his nature equally difperfed, into the greateft, and leaft actions of his too fhort life. Which Will of his, will ever remain for a witnefs to the world, that thofe fweet, and large, even dying affections in him, could no more be contracted with the narrownefs of pain, grief, or ficknefs, than any fparkle of our immortality can bee privately buried in the fhadow of death.

Here again this reftlefs foul of his (changing only the aire, and not the cords of her harmony) cals for Mufick; efpecially that fong which himfelf had intitled, *La cuiffe rompue*. Partly (as I conceive by the name) to fhew that the glory of mortal flefh was fhaken in him: and by that Mufick it felf, to fafhion and enfranchife his heavenly foul into that everlafting harmony of Angels, whereof thefe Concords were a kinde of terreftriall *Echo*: And in this fupreme, or middle Orb of Contemplations, he bleffedly went on, within a circular motion, to the end of all flefh.

The laft fcene of this Tragedy was the parting between the two brothers: the

the weaker shewing infinite strength in suppressing sorrow, and the stronger infinite weaknefs in expressing of it. So far did invaluable worthinesse, in the dying brother enforce the living to descend beneath his owne worth, and by abundance of childish tears, bewail the publique, in his particular lofs. Yea so far was his true remission of minde transformed into ejulation, that Sir *Philip,* (in whom all earthly passion did even as it were flash, like lights ready to burn out) recals those spirits together with a strong vertue, but weak voice; mildly blaming him for relaxing the frail strengths left to support him, in his finall combate of separation at hand. And to stop this naturall torrent of affection in both, took his leave, with these admonishing words:

*Love my Memorie, cherish my Friends; their Faith to me may assure you they are honest. But above all, govern your Will, and Affections,*

*Affections, by the Will and Word of your Creator; in me, beholding the end of this World, with all her Vanities.*

And with this Fare-well, defired the company to lead him away. Here this noble Gentleman ended the too fhort Scene his life; in which path, whofoever is not confident that he walked the next way to eternall reft, will be found to judge uncharitably.

Thus you fee how it pleafed God to fhew forth, and then fuddenly withdraw this precious light of our skie; and in fome fort adopted Patriot of the States-Generall. Between whom, and him, there was fuch a fympathie of affections; as they honoured that exorbitant worth in Sir *Philip*, by which time, and occafion had been like enough to metamorphofe this new Ariftocracy of theirs into their ancient, and much honoured forme of *Dukedome*. And he again applauded that univerfall ingenuitie, and profperous undertakings of theirs; over which
perchance

perchance he felt fomething in his own nature, poffible in time to become an elect Commander. So ufuall is it for all mortall conftitutions, to affect that, which infenfibly often works change in them to better, or worfe.

Now though I am not of their faith, who affirme wife men can governe the Starres; yet do I beleeve no Star-gazers can fo well prognofticate the good, or ill of all Governments, as the providence of men trained up in publique affaires may doe. Whereby they differ from Prophets only in this; that Prophets by infpiration, and thefe by confequence, judge of things to come.

Amongft which kind of Prophets, give me leave to reckon this Gentleman; who firft having, out of the credible *Almanach* of Hiftory, regiftred the growth, health, difeafe, and periods of Governments: that is to fay, when Monarchies grow ready for change, by over-relaxing, or contracting, when the ftates of few, or many continue, or forfake to be the fame: and in the conftant courfe of thefe viciffitudes, having fore-
feen

seen the easie satietie of mankinde with Religion, and Government, their naturall discontentment with the present, and aptnesse to welcome alteration: And againe, in the descent of each particular forme to her owne centre, having observed how these United Provinces had already changed from their ancient Dukedomes to Popularitie; and yet in that Popularitie, been forced to seek protection among the Monarchs then raigning; and to make perfect this judgment of his, had summ'd up the league offensive, and defensive between us, and them; even then he grew doubtfull, left this advantage would in time leave latitude for envy, and competencie, to work some kind of rent in our Union.

But when in the progresse of this prospect, he fell into a more particular consideration of their traffique, and ours: they without any native commodities (Art and diligence excepted) making themselves Masters of wealth in all Nations: We againe, by exporting our substantiall riches, to import a superfluous

perfluous maffe of trifles, to the vaine exhaufting of our home-borne ftaple commodities; he certainly concluded, that this true Philofophers ftone of traffique, which not only turned bafe mettals into gold, but made profit by Wars in their owne bofomes, would infallibly ftir up emulation in fuch lookers on, as were far from ftriving otherwife to imitate them.

And out of thefe, or the like grounds hath many times told me, that this active people (which held themfelves conftantly to their Religion, and Freedome) would at length grow from an adjective, to a fubftantive, and profperous fubfiftence. Whereas we on the other fide, dividing our felves, and waving in both, fhould firft become jealous, then ftrange to our friends, and in the end (by reconciliation with our common enemie) moderate that zeale, wherein exceffe only is the meane; and fo be forced to caft our fortunes into their armes for fupport, who are moft interefted in our difhonour, and ruine. Thefe with many other dangers (which
he

he provisionally feared) howsoever the wisdome of our Government may perchance have put off by prevention: yet were more then conjecturall in the aspect of superior, inferior, forraigne, and domestique Princes then raigning.

But suppose we could not by this Kalender comprehend the change of Aspects, and Policies in severall Kingdomes; yet we may at least therein discerne, both the judgment of this *Prometheus* concerning our selves, and the tender affection he carried to that oppressed Nation. Which respect of his they againe so well understood, as after his death the States of *Zealand* became suitors to her Majesty, & his noble friends, that they might have the honour of burying his body at the publique expence of their Government. A memorable wisdome of thankfulnesse, by well handling the dead, to encourage, and multiply faith in the living.

Which request had it been granted, the Reader may please to consider, what Trophies it is likely they would have erected over him, for posterity to admire,

mire, and what inscriptions would have been devised for eternizing his memory. Indeed fitter for a great, and brave Nation to enlarge, then the capacitie, or good will of a private, and inferior friend. For my own part I confesse, in all I have here set downe of his worth, and goodnesse; I find my self still short of that honour he deserved, and I desired to doe him.

I must therefore content my selfe with this poor demonstration of homage; and so proceed to say somewhat of the toyes, or Pamphlets, which I inscribe to his memory, as monuments of true affection between us; whereof (you see) death hath no power.

*CAP. XIV.*

WHen my youth, with favour of Court in some moderate proportion to my birth, and breeding in the activenesse of that time, gave mee opportunity of most businesse: then did

did my yet undifcouraged Genius moft affect to finde, or make work for it felf. And out of that freedom, having many times offered my fortune to the courfe of Forraigne employments, as the propereft forges to fafhion a Subject for the reall fervices of his Soveraigne; I found the returnes of thofe mif-placed endeavours to prove, both a vaine charge to my felfe, and an offenfive undertaking to that excellent Governeffe over all her Subjects duties and affections.

For inftance, how mild foever thofe mixtures of favours, and corrections were in that Princely Lady: yet to fhew that they fell heavy in croffing a young mans ends; I will onely choofe, and alleage foure out of many, fome with leave, fome without.

Firft, when thofe two mighty Armies of *Don Iohns*, and the Duke *Cafimires*, were to meet in the Low Countries; my horfes, with all other preparations being fhipped at *Dover*, with leave under her Bill affigned: Even then was I ftayed by a Princely Mandate, the Meffenger

## Sir PHILIP SIDNEY

Meſſenger Sir *Edward Dier.* Wherein whatſoever I felt, yet I appeale to the judicious Reader, whether there be any latitude left (more then humble obedience) in theſe nice caſes between duty, and ſelfeneſſe, in a Soveraignes ſervice?

After this, when Mr Secretary *Walſingham* was ſent Embaſſador, to treate with thoſe two Princes in a buſineſſe ſo much concerning Chriſtian blood, and Chriſtian Empires; then did the ſame irregular motion (which ſeldome reſts, but ſteales where it cannot trade) perſwade me, that whoſoever would venture to go without leave, was ſure never to bee ſtayed. Upon which falſe axiome (truſting the reſt to chance) I went over with Mr Secretary, unknown: But at my returne was forbidden her preſence for many moneths.

Againe, when my Lord of *Leiceſter* was ſent Generall of Her Majeſties Forces into the *Low Countries*, and had given me the command of an hundred Horſe; then I giving my humors over to good order, yet found, that neither

the

the earneſt interceſſion of this Grandee, feconded with mine own humble fute, and many other Honourable Friends of mine, could prevaile againſt the conſtant courſe of this excellent Lady with her Servants. So as I was forced to tarry behind; and for this importunity of mine to change my courſe, and feem to preferre nothing before my fervice about her: This Princeſſe of Government, as well as Kingdomes, made me live in her Court a ſpectacle of diffavour, too long as I conceived.

Laſtly, the univerſall fame of a battle to bee fought, between the prime Forces of *Henry* the third, and the religious of *Henry* the fourth, then King of *Navarre*; lifting me yet once more above this humble earth of duty, made me refolve to fee the difference between Kings prefent, and abfent in their Martiall Expeditions. So that without acquainting any creature, the Earle of *Eſſex* excepted, I ſhipped my felfe over: and at my returne, was kept from her prefence full fix moneths, and then received after a ſtrange manner. For this

this absolute Prince, to sever ill example from grace, averrs my going over to bee a secret imployment of Hers: and all these other petty exiles, a making good of that cloud, or figure, which she was pleased to cast over my absence. Protecting me to the world with the honour of her imployment, rather then she would, for examples sake, be forced either to punish mee farther, or too easily forgive a contempt, or neglect, in a Servant so near about her, as she was pleased to conceive it.

By which many warnings, I finding the specious fires of youth to prove far more scorching, then glorious, called my second thoughts to counsell, and in that Map cleerly discerning Action, and Honor, to fly with more wings then one: and that it was sufficient for the plant to grow where his Soveraignes hand had planted it; I found reason to contract my thoughts from those larger, but wandring *Horizons*, of the world abroad, and bound my prospect within the safe limits of duty, in such home services, as were acceptable to my Soveraigne.

In

In which retired view, Sir *Philip Sidney*, that exact image of quiet, and action: happily united in him, and feldome well divided in any; being ever in mine eyes, made me thinke it no fmall degree of honour to imitate, or tread in the fteps of fuch a Leader. So that to faile by his Compaffe, was fhortly (as I faid) one of the principall reafons I can alleage, which perfwaded me to fteale minutes of time from my daily fervices, and employ them in this kind of writing.

Since my declining age, it is true, that I had (for fome yeeres) more leafure to difcover their imperfections, then care, or induftry to amend them: finding in my felfe, what all men complaine of in the world, that it is more eafie to finde fault, excufe, or tolerate, then to examine, and reforme.

The workes (as you fee) are Tragedies, with fome Treatifes annexed. The Treatifes (to fpeake truly of them) were firft intended to be for every Act a Chorus: and though not borne out of the prefent matter acted, yet being the largeft fubjects I could then think upon, and

and no such strangers to the scope of the Tragedies, but that a favourable Reader might easily find some consanguinitie between them; I preferring this generall scope of profit, before the self-reputation of being an exact Artisan in that Poeticall Mystery, conceived that a perspective into vice, and the unprosperities of it, would prove more acceptable to every good Readers ends, then any bare murmur of discontented spirits against their present Government, or horrible periods of exorbitant passions among equals.

Which with humble sayles after I had once ventured upon this spreading *Ocean* of Images, my apprehensive youth, for lack of a well touched compasse, did easily wander beyond proportion. And in my old age againe, looking back on them with a fathers eye: when I considered first, how poorly the inward natures of those glorious names were expressed: then how much easier it was to excuse deformities, then to cure them; though I found reason to change their places, yet I could not find in my heart
to

to beſtow coſt, or care, in altering their light, and limited apparell in verſe.

From hence to come particularly to that Treatiſe intitled: *The Declination of Monarchy.* Let me beg leave of the favourable Reader, to beſtow a few lines more in the ſtory of this Changling, then I have done in the reſt; and yet to uſe no more ſerious authority then the rule of *Diogenes,* which was, to hang the Poſie where there is moſt need.

The firſt birth of that *Phantaſme* was divided into three parts, with intention of the Author, to be diſpoſed amongſt their fellows, into three diverſe Acts of the Tragedies. But (as I ſaid before) when upon a ſecond review, they, and the reſt were all ordain'd to change their places; then did I (like an old, and fond Parent, unlike to get any more children) take pains rather to cover the dandled deformities of theſe creatures with a coat of many ſeames, then careleſly to drive them away, as birds doe their young ones.

Yet againe, when I had in mine own caſe well weigh'd the tenderneſſe of
that

that great fubject; and confequently, the nice path I was to walke in between two extremities; but efpecially the danger, by treading afide, to caft fcandall upon the facred foundations of Monarchy; together with the fate of many Metaphyficall *Phormio's* before me, who had loft themfelves in teaching Kings, and Princes, how to governe their People: then did this new profpect dazzle mine eyes, and fufpend my travell for a time.

But the familiar felf-love, which is more or leffe born in every man, to live, and dye with him, prefently moved me to take this Bear-whelp up againe and licke it. Wherein I, rowfing my felfe under the banner of this flattery, went about (as a fond mother) to put on richer garments, in hope to adorne them. But while thefe clothes were in making, I perceived that coft would but draw more curious eyes to obferve deformities. So that from thefe checks a new counfell rofe up in me, to take away all opinion of ferioufneffe from thefe perplexed pedegrees; and to this end

end carelesly cast them into that hypocriticall figure *Ironia*, wherein men commonly (to keep above their workes) seeme to make toies of the utmost they can doe.

And yet againe, in that confusing mist, when I beheld this grave subject (which should draw reverence and attention) to bee over-spangled with lightnesse, I forced in examples of the Roman gravity, and greatnesse, the harsh severity of the *Lacedemonian* Government; the riches of the *Athenian* learning, wit, and industry; and like a man that plaies divers parts upon severall hints, left all the indigested crudities, equally applied to Kings, or Tyrants: whereas in every cleere judgement, the right line had beene sufficient enough to discover the crooked; if the image of it could have proved credible to men.

Now for the severall branches, or discourses following; they are all Members of one, and the same imperfect body, so as I let them take their fortunes (like Essayes) onely to tempt, and stir up some more free Genius, to fashion the whole

whole frame into finer mould for the worlds ufe. The firft limme of thofe Treatifes (I mean that Fabrick of a fuperftitious Church) having by her mafterfull ambition over Emperours, Kings, Princes, free States, and Councels, with her *Conclave* deceits, ftrengths, and unthankfulneffe, fpred fo far beyond my *Horizon*, as I at once gave over her, and all her derivatives to *Gamaliels* infallible cenfure; Leaving Lawes, Nobility, War, Peace, and the reft, (as glorious Trophies of our old Pope, the fin) to change, reforme, or become deformed, according as vanity, that limitleffe mother of thefe Idolatries, fhould either winne of the truth, or the truth of them.

Laftly, concerning the Tragedies themfelves; they were in their firft creation three; Whereof *Antonie* and *Cleopatra*, according to their irregular paffions, in forfaking Empire to follow fenfuality, were facrificed to the fire. The executioner, the author himfelfe. Not that he conceived it to be a contemptible younger brother to the reft: but left
while

while he seemed to looke over much upward, hee might stumble into the Astronomers pit. Many members in that creature (by the opinion of those few eyes, which saw it) having some childish wantonnesse in them, apt enough to be construed, or strained to a personating of vices in the present Governors, and government.

From which cautious prospect, I bringing into my minde the ancient Poet's metamorphosing mans reasonable nature into the sensitive of beasts, or vegetative of plants; and knowing these all (in their true morall) to bee but images of the unequall ballance between humors, and times; nature, and place. And again in the practice of the world, seeing the like instance not poetically, but really fashioned in the Earle of *Essex* then falling; and ever till then worthily beloved, both of *Queen*, and people: This sudden descent of such greatnesse, together with the quality of the Actors in every Scene, stir'd up the Authors second thoughts, to bee carefull (in his owne case) of leaving faire weather

weather behind him. Hee having, in the Earles precipitate fortune, curioufly obferved: Firft, how long this Noblemans birth, worth, and favour had been flattered, tempted, and ftung by a fwarm of Sect-animals, whofe property was to wound, and fly away: and fo, by a continuall affliction, probably enforce great hearts to turne, and toffe for eafe; and in thofe paffive poftures, perchance to tumble fometimes upon their Soveraignes Circles.

Into which pitfall of theirs, when they had once difcerned this Earle to be fallen; ftraight, under the reverend ftile of *Læfa Majeftas*, all inferiour Minifters of Juftice (they knew) would be juftly let loofe to work upon him. And accordingly, under the fame cloud, his enemies took audacity to caft Libels abroad in his name againft the State, made by themfelves; fet papers upon pofts, to bring his innocent friends in queftion. His power, by the Jefuiticall craft of rumor, they made infinite; and his ambition more then equall to it. His Letters to private men were read openly,

openly, by the piercing eyes of an Atturnies Office, which warranteth the conſtruction of every line in the worſt ſenſe againſt the writer.

My ſelfe, his Kinſman, and while I remained about the *Queen*, a kinde of *Remora*, ſtaying the violent courſe of that fatall Ship, and theſe winde-watching Paſſengers (at leaſt, as his enemies imagined) abruptly ſent away to guard a figurative Fleet, in danger of nothing, but theſe *Proſopopeia's* of inviſible rancor; and kept (as in a free Priſon) at *Rocheſter*, till his head was off.

Before which ſudden journey, caſting mine eyes upon the catching Court ayres, which I was to part from; I diſcerned my Gracious Soveraigne to bee every way ſo invironed with theſe, not *Iupiter's*, but *Pluto's* thunder-workers; as it was impoſſible for Her to ſee any light, that might lead to grace, or mercy: but many encouraging Meteors of ſeverity, as againſt an unthankfull favourite, and traiterous Subject; hee ſtanding, by the Law of *England*, condemned for ſuch.

So

So that let his heart bee (as in my confcience it was) free from this unnaturall crime, yet thefe *unreturning* fteps feemed well worth the obferving. Efpecially in the cafe of fuch a Favorite, as never put his Soveraigne to ftand between her People, and his errors; but here, and abroad placed his body in the forefront, againft all that either threatned, or affaulted Her.

And being no Admirall, nor yet a Creator of Admiralls, whereby feare, or hope might have kept thofe temporary *Neptunes* in a kinde of subjection to him; yet hee freely ventured himfelfe in all Sea-actions of his time. As if he would war the greatneffe of envy, place, and power, with the greatneffe of worth, and incomparable induftry. Neverthelefle hee wanted not judgement to difcerne, that whether they went with him, or tarried behind, they muft probably prove unequall yoke fellowes in the one; or in the other paffing curious, and carping judges over all his publike Actions.

Againe, this gallant young Earle, created

created (as it feemes) for action, before he was Martiall, firft as a private Gentleman, and after as a Lieutenant by Commiffion, went in the head of all our Land Troops, that marched in his time; and befides experience, ftill wan ground, even through competency, envy, and confufed mixtures of equality or inequality, amongft the factious Englifh, all inferiour to his owne active worth, and merit.

Laftly, he was fo far from affecting the abfolute power of *Henry* the thirds Favourites, I meane under a King to become equall at leaft with him, in creating and depofing Chancellors, Treafurers, and Secretaries of State, to raife a ftrong party for himfelfe; as he left both place, and perfons entire in their fupreme jurisdictions, or Ma- giftracies under his Soveraigne, as fhee granted them. And though hce forefaw a neceffary diminution of their peacefull predicaments by his carrying up the ftandard of *Mars* fo high, and withall knew they (like wife men) muft as certainly difcern, that the rifing of his,

or

or falling of their fcales depended upon the profperity, or unprofperity of his undertakings: yet (I fay) that active heart of his freely chofe to hazard himfelfe upon their cenfures, without any other provifionall rampier againft the envious, and fuppreffing crafts of that party, then his owne hope, and refolution to deferve well.

Neither did he (like the French Favorites of that time) ferve his own humors or neceffities, by felling feats of Juftice, Nobility, or orders of honor, till they became *Colliers pour toute befte*, to the difparagement of creating power, and difcouraging of the Subjects hope, or induftry, in attaining to advancement, or profit: But fuffered *England* to ftand alone, in her ancient degrees of freedomes, and integrities, and so referved that abfolute power of Creation facred in his Soveraigne, without any mercenary ftaine, or allay.

*CAP.*

## CAP. XV.

Now after this humble, and harmlesse desire of a meane subject, expressed in qualifying a great subjects errors, by the circumstance of such instruments, as naturally (like Bats) both flye, and prey in the darke; Let the Reader pardon me, if I presume yet againe to multiply digression upon digression, in honour of her, to whom I owe my selfe, I meane *Queen Elizabeth*: and in her name clearly to avow, that though I lament the fall of this great man in Israel, neverthelesse the truth enforceth me to confesse, that howsoever these kinds of high justice may sometimes (like the uttermost of the Law) fall heavy upon one brave spirit; yet prove they mercy to many by example: and therefore as Legall, and Royall wisedomes, ought to be honoured equally in all the differing Soveraignties through the world, of one, few or many.

And

And if this *affumpfit* muſt be granted univerſally; then how much more in the caſe of ſuch a Princeſſe, as (even while ſhe was a ſubject) left patternes that might inſtruct all ſubjects, rather to undergoe the indignation of Soveraignes with the birthright of duty, then with the mutiny of over-ſenſible, and rebellious affections; which ever (like diſeaſed pulſes) beat faſter, or ſlower then they ſhould, to ſhew all to be infected about them? Whereas this Lady, in the like ſtraines, by an humble, and conſtant temper, had already with true obedience triumphed over the curious examinations of aſcending flattery, or deſcending Tyranny, even in the tenderneſſe of Princes ſucceſſions.

And to make this manifeſt to bee choice, and not chance: even when her ſtepmother misfortune grew ripe for delivery, then was ſhe neither born crying, as children be: nor yet by the ſudden change from a priſon, to a Throne, came ſhe upon that Stage confuſedly barking after all that had offended:

offended: but like one borne to behold true light, inftantly fixeth her thoughts upon larger notions then revenge, or favour. And in the infancy of her Raigne, cals for *Benefield* her hardhearted Gaoler; bids him enjoy not a deferved, but free given peace under his narrow vine: with this affurance, that whenfoever fhe defired to have prifoners over feverely intreated, fhe would not forget to commit the cuftody of them to his charge.

Againe, for the next object, looking backward upon her fifters Raigne, fhe obferves Religion to have been changed; Perfecution, like an ill weed, fuddenly grown up to the higheft; The mercy of the infinite prefcribed, by abridgment of time, and adding torments to the death of his creatures: falvation publifhed in many more *Creeds* then fhe was taught to beleeve: A double Supremacy in one Kingdome; *Rome* become Emperour of the Clergy, and by bewitching the better halfe of man (I meane the foule) challenging both over Clergy, and Laity, the ftile of
the

the *Great God: Rex Regum, Dominus Dominantium.*

This view brought forth in her a vow, like that of the holy Kings in the Old Teftament; *viz.* that fhe would neither hope, nor feeke for reft in the mortall traffique of this world, till fhe had repaired the precipitate ruines of our *Saviours Militant Church*, through all her Dominions; and as fhe hoped, in the reft of the World, by her example. Upon which Princelike refolution, this She-*David* of ours ventured to undertake the great *Goliath* among the *Philiftins* abroad, I mean *Spain* and the *Pope*; defpifeth their multitudes, not of men, but of Hofts; fcornfully rejecteth that Holy Fathers wind-blowne fuperftitions, and takes the (almoft folitary) truth for her Leading-Star.

Yet tears fhe not the Lyons jawes in funder at once, but moderately begins with her own Changlings; gives the Bifhops a proper motion, but bounded: the Nobility time to reforme themfelves, with inward, and outward Councell; revives her Brothers Lawes for

for eftablifhing of the Churches doctrine, and difcipline, but moderates their feverity of proceeding; gives frailty, and fect, time to reforme at home: and in the mean feafon fupplyes the Prince of *Conde* with men, and money, as chief among the Proteftants in *France*; gathers, and revives the fcattered hofts of Ifrael at the worft: takes *New-Haven*, perchance with hope of redeeming *Callice*, to the end her axle-trees might once againe lie upon both fhores, as her right did: refufeth marriage, reformes and redeemes Queen *Maries* vanities, who firft glorying in the Spanifh feed, publifheth that fhe was with childe, and inftantly offers up that Royall fuppofed Iffue of hers, together with the abfolute Government of all her Natives to the mixt Tyranny of *Rome* and *Caftile*.

In which endleffe path of fervitude, the Noune adjective nature of this fuperftitious Princeffe, proceeded yet a degree further; ftriving to confirme that double bondage of people, and Pofterity, by Act of Parliament. Where
on

on the other fide, the Spanifh King, beholding thefe remiffe homages of frailty, with the unthankfull, and infatiable eyes of ambition, apprehends thefe petty facrifices, as fit ftrawes, fticks, or feathers, to be pull'd out of faint wings, for the building up, and adorning of a Conquerours neft. And under this Tyrannicall *Crifis*, takes freedome to exhauft her treafure to his owne ends, breakes our league with *France*, and in that breach fhakes the facred foundation of the reft, winnes St *Quintins*, while we loft *Callice*.

Contrary to all which thought-bound Councels of her fifter *Maries*, Queen *Elizabeth* (as I faid) not yet out of danger of her Romifh fubjects at home; threatned with their mighty faction, and party abroad; pefter'd befides with want of money, and many binding Lawes of her fifters making: yet like a Palme, under all thefe burdens, fhe raifeth her felfe Prince-like: and upon notice of her Agents difgrace abroad, his fervants being put into the Inquifition by the Spaniard; her Merchants
furprized

surprized in *America*, contrary to the league between *Charles* the fifth, and *Henry* the eighth; which gave free traffique: *In omnibus, & singulis Regnis, Dominiis, Insulis*, notwithstanding that Astronomicall, or rather biaced division of the world by the Popes lines, which (contrary to the nature of all lines) only keep latitude for the advantage of *Spain:* She (I say) upon these insolencies, receives the *Hollander*, and protects him from persecution of the Duke of *Alva:* settles these poore Refugees in *Norwich, Colchester, Sandwich, Maidstone*, and *South-Hampton*.

Yet againe, when this faith-distinguishing Duke appealed to her selfe: she binding her heart for better, or worse, to the words of her Contract; summons these afflicted strangers to depart. Their number was great, their time short, and yet their weather-beaten soules so sensible of long continued oppressions in their liberties, and consciences, as (by the opportunity of this Ostracisme) they in their passage surprized *Brill, Flushing*, and diverse other Towns, expulsing the
Spaniards;

Spaniards; and by this brave example, taught, and proclaimed a way of freedome to all well affected Princes, and Provinces, that were oppreſt.

Wherein it may pleaſe the Reader to obſerve, that *Henry* the third of *France*, being one in the ſame League, and belike upon change of heart, which ever brings forth new queſtions, demanding, whether *mutuall defence againſt all*, extended to the cauſe of Religion? was preſently anſwered by her; that ſhe both treated, and concluded in the ſame ſenſe; and if it were required at her hands, would performe every branch of it to her uttermoſt. The *French King* hereupon makes war with the Proteſtants: *Monſieur* his brother ſecretly protects them by *Caſimire*.

Againe about that time, at the requeſt of the *Spaniſh* King, ſhe guards his Navy into *Flanders*; where it being loſt, and ſhe requeſted by the ſame King to lend him her owne Ships, for recovery of the Maritime Townes fallen from him: this bleſſed *Lady* both denyes this crafty requeſt of a Conqueror, and withall providently

providently refuseth any of his ships to be harboured in her Ports. Yet in honour of her ancient League with the House of *Burgundy*, she publisheth the like inhibition to her beloved, and safe Neighbours the *Netherlands*. And instantly, with a strong judgment in ballancing of forraigne Princes, perswades the King of *Spain* to make peace with the *Hollanders*, and on the other side disswades those distressed *Hollanders* from joyning with *France*. As I conceive, thinking that Kingdome (manumised from us by time) might through the conjunction of the *Holland* shipping, and Mariners, with their disciplin'd Land-Armies of horse and foot, prove more dangerous enemies, either by way of invasion, or incursion (as I said once before) then that Kings glorious Standard, borne among his barbed horse, and light foot had hitherto done, either in our entised undertakings, or abandoned retraits.

Besides it is worthy of reverence in this *Queen*, that she never was afraid, or ashamed to averre the quarrell of Religion

ligion for a ground of her friends, or enemies.

And though in the charity of a Chriſtian Prince, even in the danger of a growing faction at home, ſhe was content to let devout conſcience live quietly in her Realmes: yet when they began to practiſe diſunion in the Church, as their Jeſuited ſpirits naturally affect to doe: Then to ſhew that ſhe was as well ſervant to God, as by him King over Peoples, ſhe tyed the head of the ſacrifice perchance a little cloſer to the hornes of the altar. And made thoſe ſpirits which would not know the true God altogether, to have ſome kinde of ſenſe, or ſmart of his Religious Lawes; howſoever they were dead, and ſacrificed to the growing Supremacy of the Roman Miter, or conquering Scepter of *Spaine*; ordain'd (as ſhe thought) by exceſſe of playing faſt or looſe with God, and the world; in time, one to devoure the other; ambitious and ſuperſtitious ſubtleties being an Abyſſe, or Sea, where the ſtronger infallibly devoures the weaker.

She makes a publique League, for defence

defence of Religion, with the King of *Scots*, *Denmark*, and the Princes of *Germany*; perſwades a Marriage between *Scotland* and *Denmark*; exileth all Jeſuites, and Seminary Prieſts by Act of Parliament; makes it felony to harbor any of them in *England*, or for the Engliſh to ſend any of theirs beyond the Seas, to be trained up among them.

Upon the loſſe of *Antuerpe*, ſhe reſolutely undertakes the protection of the Netherlanders, and to diſtract the Spaniard (as I ſaid before) ſends *Drake* to the *Weſt-Indies*, with 21 Ships, who ſurpriſed *Domingo*, and *Cartagena*. And immediately after his returne, with ſpoile, and triumph (to prevent all poſſibility of Invaſion) ſhe ſets him to Sea againe, with Commiſſion to burne all Ships, Gallyes, and Boats, along his Spaniſh Coaſts. Who, in the ſame Voyage, breaks through diverſe of his Gallyes in the Bay of *Cales*, appointed to withſtand him; takes, burnes, and drownes 100 Sayle laden with munition, and victuals. From thence in his way to *Capo* St *Vincent*, he ſurpriſeth three Forts:

burnes

burnes ſhips, fiſher-boats, and nets; and then making for the *Azores*, hee there takes a Carricke comming from the *Eaſt-Indies*.

The next yeare (as treading in his ſteps) *Cavendiſh* returnes from his journey about the world, with the ſpoile of nineteen Ships, and of many ſmall Towns in *America*.

This and ſuch like providence did this miracle of Princes uſe in all her Wars, whereby her Wars maintained her wealth, and that wealth ſupplyed her War. So as ſhe came ever in ſtate, when ſhe demanded aid from her Houſe of Commons. Neither did ſhe fetch, or force preſidents from her Predeceſſors in thoſe demands: but made her ſelf a preſident to all Poſterities, that the love of people to a loving Princeſſe is not ever curiouſly ballanced, by the ſelf-pittying abilities of mankinde: but their ſpirits, hearts, and ſtates being drawne up above their owne fraile ſelfneſſe, the audit is taken after; and perchance ſumm'd up with a little ſmart to themſelves, wherein they glory.

Neither

Neither did she, by any curious search after Evidence to enlarge her Prerogatives Royall, teach her subjects in Parliament, by the like self-affections, to make as curious inquisition among their Records, to colour any encroaching upon the sacred Circles of Monarchy: but left the rise or fall of these two ballances asleep, with those aspiring spirits, who (by advantage of state, or time taken) had been authors of many biaced motions: And in some confused Parliaments amongst the Barons Wars, even forced her Ancestors, with one breath, to proscribe and restore; to call out of the House of Commons, by Writ, to the upper House, during the Session: Wherein one mans sudden advancement proves envious to foure hundred of his equals; and from the same, not truly active, but rather passive vaine, to imprison and release unjudicially, sometime striving to master the multitude, by their Nobility, then again waving the Nobility with the multitude of people; both marks of disease, and no healthfull state in a Monarchy. All which she providently

providently forefaw, and avoided; left, by the like infenfible degrees of mifleading paffions, fhe might be conftrained to defcend, and labour the compaffing of diforderly ends, by a Mechanicall kinde of Univerfity Canvaffe.

So that this bleffed, and bleffing *Lady*, with a calme minde, as well in quiet, as ftirring times, ftudied how to keep her ancient under-earth buildings, upon their firft well laid foundations. And if fhe found any ftray'd, rather to reduce them back to their originall circuits, then fuffer a ftep to be made over, or befides thofe time-authorized affemblies. And by this refervedneffe, ever comming upon the ftage a Commander, and no Petitioner, fhe preferv'd her ftate above the affronts of Nobility, or people; and according to birthright, ftill became a foveraigne Judge over any dutifull, or encroaching petitions of Nobles, or Commons.

For this *Lady*, though not prophetically, yet like a provident Princeffe, in the feries of things, and times, forefaw through the long lafting wifdome of
Government,

Government, a quinteſſence, howſoever abſtracted out of Morall Philoſophy, and humane Lawes, yet many degrees in uſe of mankinde above them. She, I ſay, foreſaw, that every exceſſe of paſſion expreſt from the Monarch in Acts, or Councels of Eſtate, would infallibly ſtir up in the people the like cobwebs of a popular ſpinning, and therefore from theſe piercing grounds, ſhe concluded, that a ſteady hand in the government of Soveraignty, would ever prove more proſperous, then any nimble or witty practiſe, crafty ſhifting, or Imperious forcing humors poſſibly could doe.

Againe in the latitudes which ſome moderne Princes allow to their Favorites, as ſupporters of Government, and middle wals between power, and the peoples envy; it ſeems this *Queen* reſervedly kept entrenched within her native ſtrengths, and Scepter.

For even in the height of *Eſſex* his credit with her, how far was ſhe from permitting him (like a *Remus*) to leap over any wall of her new-built Anti-Rome;

Rome; or with a young, and unexperienced *genius* to shuffle Pulpits, Parliaments, Lawes, and other fundamentall establishments of her Kingdomes, into any glorious apparances of will, or power? It should seem foreseeing, that howsoever this unexpected racking of people might for a time, in some particulars, both please, and adde a glossy stick to enlarge the Eagles nest; yet that in the end all buildings above the truth, must necessarily have forced her two *Supremacies*, of state, and nature, to descend, and through irregularities acted in her name, either become a sanctuary between the world, and inferior persons errors; or (as playing an after-game with her subjects, for a subject) constraine her to change the tenure of commanding power, into a kind of unprincely mediation. And for what? Even vainly to intreat her people, that they would hope well of diverse confusions: howsoever they might seem heady, nay ignorant passions: and such as threatned no lesse, then a losse of native Liberties, descended upon her people,

people, by the fame prefcription of time and right, by which the Crowne had defcended upon her felfe, and her Anceftors; with a probable confequence of many more fharp pointed Tyrannies over them and their freedomes, then their happily deceafed Parents ever tafted or dream't of.

Befides, admit thefe flatterings, and threatnings of hope, or feare (which tranfcendent power is fometimes forced to worke by) could have drawne this excellent Princeffe, and her time-prefent fubjects to make braffe an equally currant ftandard with gold, or filver, within her Sea-compafs'd Dominions; yet abroad, where the freedome of other Soveraignties is bounded by Religion, Juftice, and well-waigh'd commerce amongft Neighbor-Princes, fhe forefaw, the leaft thought of multiplying felf-Prerogatives there, would inftantly be difcredited and reflected back to ftir up difcouragement in the fofteft hearts, of her moft humble and dutifull fubjects.

Therefore contrary to all thefe captived,

tived, and captiving apparances, this experienced Governeſſe of ours publiſhed to the world, by a conſtant *Series* in her actions, that ſhe never was, nor ever would be overloaden with any ſuch exceſſes in her Perſon, or defects in her Government, as might conſtraine her to ſupport, or be ſupported by a Monopolous uſe of Favourites; as if ſhe would make any greater then her ſelfe, to governe Tyrannically by them.

Nay more; ſo far off was ſhe from any lukewarmneſſe in Religion, as if a ſingle teſtimony may have credit, that bleſſed *Queens* many and free diſcourſes with my ſelfe, ingeniouſly bare record; that the unexpected converſion of *Henry* the Fourth fell fatally upon him, by the weakneſſes of his Predeceſſor *Henry* the Third, and the diſſolute miſcarriage of his Favourites. Who like Lapwings, with the ſhels of authority about their necks, were let looſe to runne over all the branches of his Kingdome, miſleading Governors, Nobility, and People from the ſteady, and mutuall reſt of Lawes, Cuſtomes, and other ancient wiſ-

domes

domes of government, into the wilderneſſes of ignorance, and violence of will. Amongſt which defects, all fundamentall changes (eſpecially of Religion) in Princes would be found (as ſhe conceived) the true diſcipline of Atheiſme amongſt their Subjects; all ſacrifices, obedience excepted, being but deare-bought knowledges of the Serpent, to expulſe Kings, and People once againe out of Mediocrity, that reciprocall Paradiſe of mutuall humane duties. Prophetically concluding, that whoſoever will ſell God to purchaſe earth, by making that eternall unity of many ſhapes, muſt in the end make him of none: and ſo bee forced with loſſe, contempt and danger to traffique not for an heires place, but a younger brothers; in that Church, at whoſe wide gates he had (with ſhame enough) already turned in. And under conditions of a Servant, rather then of a Sonne, be conſtrained for his firſt ſtep to ſet up the Jeſuits faction, providently ſuppreſſed by himſelfe before, and therein to ſhake the *Sorboniſts*, faithfull ſupporters

porters in all times of Crowne-Soveraignty, againſt theſe ſlave-making conjunctions betweene the Spaniard, and his *Chaplaine*. Nay, yet with a greater ſhew of ingratitude, his next ſtep muſt be to ſuppreſſe thoſe humble ſoules, who had long ſupported him, whileſt he was King of *Navarre*, againſt that murthering Holy water of Spaniſh *Rome*. Laſtly, to ſhew that no power can reſt upon a ſteep, hee muſt precipitately be forced to ſend Embaſſadors to *Rome* (with his Sword in his ſcabbard) ſervily begging mercy, and grace of ſuch reconciled enemies, whoſe endleſſe ends of ſpirituall, and temporall Supremacy (this Princeſſe knew) would never forgive any heavenly Truth, or earthly power that ſhould oppoſe their Combination. Finally ſhe concluded that holy Church of *Rome* to be of ſuch a *Bucephalus* nature, as no Monarch ſhall be ever able to beſtride it, except onely the ſtirring *Alexanders* of time preſent, wherein the world is paſſing finely overſhot in her own bow.

Wherefore to end, (as I began) with the

the case of *Essex*, was not this excellent Princesse therein a witnesse to her selfe, that she never chose, or cherished Favourite, how worthy soever, to Monopolize over all the spirits, and businesse of her Kingdome; or to imprison the universall counsels of nature, and State, within the narrownesse of a young fraile mans lustfull, or unexperienced affections? Not thinking any one, especially a Subject, better able to doe all then her selfe. Where like a worthy head of a great body, she left the Offices, and Officers of the Crowne free to governe in their owne Predicaments, according to her trust. Reserving appeales to her selfe, as a Sea-mark to warn all Creatures under her that shee had still a creating, or defacing power inherent in her Crown and Person, above those subalterne places by which shee did minister universall justice. And though her wisdom was too deep to nurse or suffer faction amongst those great Commanders, and distributers of Publique Rights: yet was shee as carefull not to permit any Aristocraticall cloud,

cloud, or pillar, to shew, or shadow forth any superstitious, or false lights between her and her people.

## CAP. XVI.

AGaine in her houshold affaires she kept the like equall hands ballancing the sloth or sumptuousnesse of her great Stewards, and white staves, with the providence, and reservednesse of a Lord Treasurer, kept up the Tables for Servants, Sutors, and for honors sake in her owne house; not suffering publike places to be made particular farmes of private men, or the honor of her houshold to be carried into theirs: And withall, by the same reverend Auditor, shee watched over the nimble Spirits, selfe-seeking or large-handednesse of her active Secretaries; examining their Intelligence, money, Packets, Bils of transportation, Propositions of State, which they offer'd up by their places, together with Sutes of other

other Nature, in her wifdome ftill fevering the reall bufineffe from the fpecious but narrow felfneffe of inferior Officers.

Befides, all thefe were examined by reverend Magiftrates, who having bin formerly iffuers of her Majefties Treafure in the Secretaries places, did now worthily become Governours of her Finances, as beft able to judge between the felfneffe of place, or perfon, and the reall neceffities of her State, and Kingdome. A fine art of Government by well chofen Minifters fucceffively to wall in her Exchequer from the vaft expence of many things, efpecially upon Forraigne Ambaffadors, which (fhe knew) could neither bring reverence, nor thankfulneffe to their Soveraigne.

Under which head of Forraigne, and Domeftique Ambaffadors, the anfwer wherewith that Majefticall Lady entertained the *Polacke*, expected a treating Ambaffador, but proving (as fhe told him) a defying Herald, is never to be forgotten among Princes, as an inftance how fenfible they ought to be of indignity,

dignity, and how ready to put off fuch fudden affronts, without a prompting of Councellors; againe worthily memorable among her Subjects, as a demonftrative argument that fhe would ftill referve *Mofes* place entire to her felfe amongft all the diftributions of *Iethro*.

And to go on with her Domeftique affaires how provident was fhe, out of the like caution, and to the fame end, that even hee who overfaw the reft, might have his owne greatneffe overfeen, and limited too. Whereupon fhe forgot not to allay that vaft power and jurisdiction of her Treafurers Office, with inferior Officers of her Finances, and perchance under an active Favourits eyes, kept her owne; Befides fhe watched and checked him in his marriage made with *Paulet* his Predeceffor, referved that mans accounts, and arrears as a rod over his Grandchilds alliance, qualified, and brought the fines of his many, and great Copyholds to eafie rates, would never fuffer any propofition to take hold of uniting the Dutchy of *Lancafter* to her Exchequer, what narrow reafons foever were

were alleaged of sparing and cutting off the multiplicity of Officers, with their wages and ignorances or corruptions, all chargable, and cloudy paths, which the dealing with Princes moneys doth as naturally bring forth, as *Africa* doth Monsters. But like a provident Soveraigne, knowing that place in a Monarchy must help as well to traine up servants, as to reward, and encourage merit; she constantly (to that end) keeps that Chancellorship of the Dutchy entire, and will not make the rewarding part of her Kingdome lesse, to overload her Exchequer with any addition of instrumentall gaine amongst under Officers, into whose barns those harvests are inned for the most part.

Again with the same caution in all her doings she made merit precious, honour dainty, and her graces passing rare, keeping them (as the Venetians doe their curiously refined gold) to set an edge upon the industry of man, and yet (like branches of Creation) sparingly reserved within the circuit of her Throne, as inherent, and tender Prerogatives,
not

not fit to be left at randome in the power of ambitious Favourites, or low-looking Councellors, whofe ends are feldome fo large, or fafe for the publique, as the native Princes Councels are, or ought to be.

For her Clergy with their Ecclefiafticall, or Civill jurisdictions, fhe fafhioned the Arches, and Weftminfter Hall to take fuch care one to bound another, that they in limiting themfelves, enlarged her Royalties, as the chiefe and equall foundations of both their greatneffes; fhe gave the fuperior places freely, left by example fhe fhould teach them to commit fymony with their inferiors, and fo adde fcandall in ftead of reputation to Gods Word, whofe allowed Meffengers they affect to feem.

Her Parliaments fhe ufed, to fupply her neceffarily expended treafure, and withall, as Maps of orders, or diforders, through her whole Kingdome. In which reverend Body (as I faid before) fhe ftudied not to make parties, or faction, advancing any prefent Royallift out of the nether

nether Houfe, to ftir up envy upon her felf amongft all the reft, and fo publifh the Crowne to ufe perfonall practifes of hope, or feare, in thefe generall Councels of her Kingdome, but by forbearing art was never troubled with any artificiall brickwals from them; fo as their need and fears concurring with her occafions, made their defires and counfels concurre too, and out of thofe equall, and common grounds forced every man to beleeve his private fifh-ponds could not be fafe, whiles the publique ftate of the Kingdome ftood in danger of prefent, or expectant extremities.

Her Councell-board (as an abridgment of all other jurifdictions) fhe held up in due honour, propounded not her great bufineffes of State to them with any prejudicate refolution, which once difcovered, fuppreffeth the freedome both of fpirit and judgment, but opens her felfe clearly, heares them with refpect; obferves number, and reafon, in their voices, and makes a quinteffence of all their concords, or difcords within her felfe, from whence the refolutions

and

and directions came fuddenly, and fecretly forth for execution.

To be fhort, fhe kept awe ftirring over all her Courts, and other imployments, as her antidote againft any farther neceffity of punifhments ; In which arts of men, and Government, her nature, education, and long experience, had made her become excellent above both Sexes.

Againe, for the Regiment of her Grandees at home, fhe did not fuffer the Nobility to be fervants one to another, neither did her Gentry weare their Liveries as in the Ages before ; their number and wealth was moderate, and their fpirits and powers counterpoifed with her Majefty, from being Authors of any new Barons Wars, and yet referved as brave halfe paces between a Throne and a people.

Her Yeomendry, a ftate under her Nobles, and above her Peafants (proper to England) fhe maintained in their abilities, and never gave them caufe to fufpect, fhe had any intent, with extraordinary Taxes out of the courfe of
Parliaments,

Parliaments, infenfibly to impoverifh & make Boors, or flaves of them, knowing that fuch a kind of champion countrey, would quickly ftir up the Nobility it felfe, to become doubtfull of their owne fences, and by confequence in danger, not only of holding lives, lands, goods, and Liberties at their Soveraignes indefinite pleafure, but by fufpence of thofe nurfing, and protecting Parliaments, to have all other native birthrights, *viz.* Pulpits, Lawes, Cuftomes, Voyces of Appeale, Audits of Trade, humble, and reverent mention of Coronation-oaths; legall publifhers, and maintainers of War, true Maps of Difeafes, and cures through her Kingdome, with many other mutuall ciments of honour, and ufe, between Soveraigne, and subjects, like to be confounded, or at leaft metamorphofed into Prerogative Taxes, wherein the people neither have voyces, nor valuable returne. I fay, this homeborne Princeffe of ours making her profpect over thefe wildernefles of will, and power, providently for her felfe, and happily for us, refufed the broad branch

of

of *Pythagoras* *Y*, and chofe that narrower, but fafer medium of State-affemblies, concluding that thefe two Honourable Houfes, were the only judicious, faithfull, and induftrious Favorites of unincroaching Monarchs.

So that it appears fhe did not affect, nor yet would be drawne (like many of her ancient Neighbours the French Kings) to have her fubjects give away their wealth after a new fafhion, *viz.* without returne of Pardons, eafe of grievances, or comfort of Lawes, left her loving people might thereby dream of fome fecret intent to indennize their lives, wealth, and freedomes, into a fhip of *Athens*, of which the name being old, and all riders, fleepers, and other Timbers new, they were to be fhipped downe a ftreame of the like nature ever, and yet never the fame. Befides not to be fhipped into that fhip as Mariners, Souldiers, Saylors, or Factors, but rather as flaves, or conquered Out-Laws, with great difhonour to the Legall, and Royall ftate of Monarchicall Government, as fhe conceived. From which
example

example of chafte power, we that live after this excellent Lady, may with great honour to her afhes refolve, that fhe would have been as averfe from bearing the envy of printing any new Lines of Taxe, Impofitions, Proclamations, or Mandats (without Parliaments) upon her ancient cœleftiall, or terreftriall Globes, as her humble subjects poffibly could be, or wifh her to be.

Now if we fhall examine the reafon of her cutting between Lawes, Kings powers, and the Peoples freedome, by fo even a thread, what can it be, but a long and happy defcent within the pedegrees of active Princes, together with the moderating education of Kings children in thofe times; or laftly in a quinteffence of abilities, gathered out of thofe bleffed, and bleffing mixtures of Nature, Education, and Practice, which never faile to lift up man above man, and keep him there, more then place or power fhall by any other encroaching advantages ever be able to doe.

In which Map, as in a true perfpective

fpective glaffe, this provident Princeffe feeing both her owne part, and her peoples, fo equally, nay advantagioufly already divided, and difpofed, fhee thought it both wifdome, and juftice to leave them ballanced, and diftinguifhed as fhe found them; Concluding that the leaft change of *Parallels*, or *Meridian* Lines newly drawne upon any the ancient Globes of Monarchall Government in abfence of Parliaments, would (like the fervice of God in an unknown Language) prove prophaned, or mif-underftood; And confequently regifter fuch a Map of writing, and blotting; of irregular raifing, and depreffing; dif-advantagious matching of things reall, and humours together, as muft multiply Atheifme in humane duties, caft trouble upon her Eftate for want of reverence at home, and provoke this heavy cenfure through all the world (*Spaine* only excepted) that fhe endeavoured the raifing of an invifible Tyrant above the Monarch; and to that end had made this ftep over Lawes, and Cuftomes into fuch a dangerous kind

kind of ignorant, and wandring confusion, as would quickly enforce mankinde, either to live like exhausted creatures, deprived of Sabbaths, or like barren earth without priviledge of any Jubile, which metamorphosing prospect (as she thought) would resemble *Circes* guests, transforme her people into divers shapes of beasts; wherin they must lose freedome, goods, fortune, language, and kinde, all at once.

An inchanted confusion imaged by the Poets, to warne Princes, that if they will easily be induced to use these racks of wit, and power indefinitly, and thereby force a free people into a despairing estate, they must even in the pride of their Governments, looke in some sort to be forced againe, either to sacrifice these *Empsons*, and *Dudleyes*, as the most popular act such Princes can doe, or else with the two edged sword of Tyranny, irregularly to climbe a degree yet higher then the truth, to maintaine these Caterpillars in eating, or offering up Religion, Lawes, &c. to the covetous, cruell, or wanton

wanton excesses of encroaching Tyranny, as though God had made all the world for one.

Nay more it pleafed this provident Queen even curioufly to forefee, what face her eftate was like to carry, if thefe biaced humours fhould continue any long raigne over us, *viz.* contempt to be caft over the Majefty of the Crown, feare among the people, hate and envy againft the reverend Magiftrate, entifement of domeftique fpirits to mutiny, or forraigne to invade upon any occafion, the Court it felfe becomming a Farme, manured by drawing up, not the fweate, but even the browes of humble fubjects; and laftly the Councell-boord, that glorious type of Civill Government, compelled to defcend, and become Broker for money, executioner of extremity, better acquainted with the Merchant, or mechanicall fcraping Revenues of ficke, and exhaufted Kingdomes, then forraigne Treaties, equall ballances of Trade, true grounds of Manufactures, myfteries of Importation, and Exportation, differing ftrengths, and weaknefles of Crownes,

alteration

alteration of Factions, or parties with advantage, danger of alliances made to the benefit of the ſtronger, the ſteady (though ſometimes intermittent) undertakings of the Conqueror, with all things elſe that concerne *Magnalia Regni*, and ſo apt inſtruments, not reverently to ſhew Princes the truth, but rather ſelf-loving creatures full of preſent and ſervile flatteries, even to the ruine of that Eſtate wherein they have and enjoy their honours.

Which confuſion of place and things being cleerly imaged within her, perſwaded this Lady to reſtrain the ſlaviſh Liberties of Tranſcendency, within Lawes, and Parliaments, as two unbatter'd Rampires againſt all overwreſtings of power, or mutinies of people, and out of theſe grounds to conclude Prince-like, with her forefathers, that *superſtructiones antiquæ nec facilè evertuntur, nec solæ ruunt.* In this axiome making manifeſt to the world, that Time-preſents children, with their young, and unexperienced capacities, are much too narrow moulds, for any large branches of well-founded Monarchies

Monarchies to be altered, or new fashioned in, the new and old seldome matching well together, let the Ciment of seeming wisdome on either side appeare never so equall.

Now for the right use of these high pillars, if we shall descend to inferior functions, we there find her (like a working soule in a healthfull body) still all in all, and all in every part. For with the same restraining providence, she kept the Crowne from necessity to use Imperiall, and chargable Mandates upon her people, when she had most need of their service, contrary to the wisdome of all Government; Neither did she by mistaking, or misapplying instances (gathered out of the fatall conquests of her Ancestors) parallell her present need, and Levies with theirs, but wisely considered that the King, and the people were then equally possessors of both Realmes, and so in all impositions contributers to themselves at the first hand.

From which grounds, like a contented and a contenting Soveraigne, she acknowledged these differences to be reall, and accordingly

accordingly by an equall audit taken from her itinerant Judges, with the Juftices inhabiting in every County, after fhe was well informed of her fubjects abilities, and her enemies threatnings, fhe then, by advice of her Privy Councell fummon'd her Parliaments, demanded ayd, and was never refufed; In returne of which loving and free gifts, fhe difpofed thofe extraordinary helps to the repayring, and provifionall fupplying of her Forts along the Coaft, with offenfive and defenfive munitions, fhe ftored her Office of the Ordnance as a royall Magazine to furnifh the whole Kingdom in extremity, and when there were no wars, yet fhe kept it full, as an equall pledge of ftrength, and reputation, both abroad, and at home.

Laftly, this Princeffe being confident in thefe native Sea-walls of ours, fit to beare moving Bulwarkes in martial times, and in Civill Traffiques to carry out, and in, all Commodities with advantage; fhe double ftored her Navy Magazines with all materials, provided before-hand for fuch workes, and things,
as

## Sir PHILIP SIDNEY 199

as required time, and could not be bought with money; befides, fhe furnifhed her Sea Arfinals with all kind of ftaple provifions, as Ordnance, Pitch, Rofin, Tar, Mafts, Deale boards, Cordage, &c. for the building, and maintaining of her Navie, flourifhing in multitude of Ships for War and Trade.

And as the life of that vaft body, fhe for encreafe of Mariners, gave Princely countenance to all long voyages, knowing they would neceffarily require Ordnance, men, munition, and burthen; and further to encourage this long-breathed worke, fhe added out of her Exchequer an allowance of fo much in the tun for the builders of any fhips upward of fo many hundred Tuns; She cherifhed the fifher-boats with priviledges along her Coafts, as nurferies of Sea-men; brought *Groniland*, and *Newfound-land* fifhing in reputation to encreafe her ftock of Mariners, both by taking, and tranfporting what they took far off.

And for the Governours of her Navy under the Admirall, as well in times of peace as war, fhe chofe her principall Officers

Officers out of the gallanteſt Sea Commanders of that time, whoſe experience ſhe knew taught them how to husband and guide her *Muſcovy* Company in generall Proviſions, not as partner with her Merchants in building, but reſtraining the Ship-keepers riot, or expence in harbour, and at Sea, how to furniſh, or martiall ſhips, and Mariners in all kind of Sea-fights to their beſt advantage.

Beſides, through the ſame mens judgments, ſhe made all directions paſs for the divers moulds required in ſhipping betweene our Seas, and the Ocean, as the drawth of water, high, or low, diſpoſing of ports, cleanly roomes for Victuals, convenience of Deckes for Fight, or Trade, ſafe conveyance for Powder, & all other munition, fit Stowage of Sea ſtores, according to the difference of heats, or colds in the Climes they were to reſide in, or paſſe through.

Againe, as well to inſtruct the Captaines in their particular duties, as to keep a hand of Government over the large truſt, and charge committed to them,

them, in all expeditions, the Ship with her furniture, tackling, and men, the Gunners Roome with all munition of that kind, the Boat-fwains provifion of Anchors, Cables, Canvas, and Sea-ftores, the Purfers, Stewards, and Cooks Roomes touching victuals were delivered to the Captaines by Bill indented; the one part kept with the Officers of the Navy at home, the other in the hands of every private Captaine to examine his accounts by when he return'd: of which my felfe am witneffe, as being well acquainted with the ufe of it in my youth, but utterly unacquainted with the change fince, or any reafons of it.

Laftly, this great Governeffe could tell how to worke her high Admirals (without noife) to refign their Patents, when the courfe of times made them in power, and gaine, feeme, or grow too exorbitant; yet kept fhe up their Command at Sea, and when they were there made them a limited, or abfolute Commiffion under the great Seale of *England*, fometimes affociating, and qualifying their place, with a Councell
of

of war of her own choice, and ever guiding the generalities of the Voyage with inftructions proper to the bufinefs, and to be publifhed at Sea in a time prefixed.

Out of which caution in her principall expeditions, fhe ftriving (as I faid) to allay that vaft power of place with fome infenfible Counterpoife, many times joyned an active Favourite with that Sea *Neptune* of hers, making credit, place, and merit, finely competitors in her fervice; Befides, fhe well underftanding the humours of both, temper'd them fo equally one with another in her latter expeditions, as the Admirall being remiffe, and apt to forgive all things, *Effex* feverely true to Martiall Difcipline, and loath to wound it by forgiving petty errours under that implacable Tyrant *Mars*, in all likelihood her Fleet could hardly be over failed, or under ballafted, and confequently the Crowne (in her abfence) was fure to be guarded with more eyes than two, to prevent confufion in Martiall Affaires, where every Ship proves beyond the
amendment

amendment of second thoughts, and so fatall to that state which paies, and negligently ventures.

The Merchant-part of her Kingdome was oppressed with few impositions, the Companies free to choose their owne Officers, to fashion their Trade, assisted with the name and countenance of her Embassadors, the custome, and returne of their industry, and adventures, contenting them in a free Market without any nearer cutting of peoples industry to the quick.

The *Flushingers,* and *Dunkerkers* in succession of time, it is true, did much afflict their Traffique, though with smal strength; whereupon she first travelled to suppresse them by force, but found the Charge grow infinite, and the cure so casuall, as she joyned Treaty with the Sword, and set her Seas by that providence, and industry, once againe at liberty from all molestation, or danger of Pyrates.

Her Universities were troubled with few *Mandates,* the *Colledges* free in all their Elections, and governed by their
own

own Statutes, the groſſe neglect of uſing the Latine Tongue ſhe ſtudied to reforme, as well for honour of the Univerſities, as for her own ſervice in all Treaties with Forraign Princes, ſhe ſtudied to multiply her *Civilians* with little charge, and yet better allowance to their Profeſſion.

In a word, ſhe preſerved her Religion without waving, kept both her Martiall, and Civill Government intire above neglect, or practice, by which, with a multitude of like inſtances, ſhe manifeſted to the World, that the well governing of a Princes own Inheritances, is (in the cleare houſe of Fame) ſuperiour to all the far noiſed conqueſts of her over-griping Anceſtors, ſince what Man lives, converſant in the *Calenders* of eſtates, but muſt know, that had not theſe wind-blown conqueſts of ours happily been ſcattered, they muſt in time have turned the moderate wealth, and degrees of *England* into the naſty poverty of the French peaſants; brought home Mandates inſtead of Lawes, waved our freedomes in Parliaments with new chriſtned chriftned Impofitions, and in the end have fubjected native and active *Albion* to become a Province, and fo inferior to her owne dearly bought forraign conquefts, being forced to yeeld up the fuperlative works of power, to the equall Laws of Nature, which almoft every where (*America* excepted) proclames the greater to be naturally a Law-giver over the leffe.

## CAP. XVII.

YEt as this wife and moderate Governeffe was far from incroaching upon any other Princes Dominions, fo wanted fhe neither forefight, courage nor might, both to fuppreffe all infolencies attempted againft her felfe, and to fupport her Neighbours unjuftly oppreffed, whereof by the Readers patience I will here adde fome few inftances.

She had no fooner perfected her Virgin-triumph over that fanctified, and

and invincible Navy, and by that loſſe publiſhed the Spaniſh ambition, weakneſſe, and malice to all Chriſtendome, ſecured her owne eſtate, revived the Netherlands, confuted the Pope, turned the caution of the Italian Princes the right way, and amazed the world; but even then to purſue that victory, and prevent her enemies ambition, which ſtill threatned the world with new Fleets; then (I ſay) did this active Lady conclude, with adviſe of her Councell, and applauſe of her Kingdome, to defend her ſelfe thenceforth by invading, and no more attend the Conquerors pleaſure at her owne doores.

Out of which reſolution ſhe firſt ſent forth the Earle of *Cumberland,* who attempted the ſurprize of *Porto Ricco,* accompliſhed it with honour, and ſo might have kept it, had not diſeaſe, and diſorder proved more dangerous enemies to him, then the great name, and ſmall force of the Spaniſh did.

Againe to prevent danger, not in the bud, but root, ſhe tooke upon her the protection of *Don Antonio* King of *Portugall,*

*gall*, sent Sir *Iohn Norris*, and Sir *Francis Drake*, with a Royall Fleet, and eleven thousand men to land, seconded with the fortune, and countenance of the Earle of *Essex*; they tooke the base Towne of the Groyne, and when they had overthrowne all that came to succour it, and burnt the Countrey, then marched they on to *Lisbone*, and in that journey sacked *Peniche*, wasted Villages, and Provinces, entred the suburbs of *Lisbone* even to the gates of the High Towne, and burnt threescore Spanish hulkes full of provisions.

And to the same end, she did, and still meant succesively to maintaine a Fleet of her owne Ships, and her fast friends the Netherlands upon his Coasts, not only to disturbe the returne of victuals, munition, and materials for War, with which the Empire, Poland, and the Hanse Townes did usually, and fatally (even to themselves) furnish this growing Monarch, but withall to keep his Navy which was riding, and building in many havens, from possibility of getting head in any one place to annoy
her;

her; and thirdly to fet fuch a Taxe upon the wafting home of his Indian Fleets, as might (in fome meafure) qualifie that fearfull abundance which elfe was like enough to fpread infection through the foundeft Councels, and Councellors of all his Neighbour-Princes.

In the meane time, the French King *Henry* the third (heartned by her example, and fucceffe) did encounter the *Guifards*, a ftrong Faction depending upon *Spaine*. And when he was made away by treafon, & the Leaguers in Armes under the Spaniards protection, then did the Queen providently take opportunity to change the Seat of her Warres, and affifted *Henry* the fourth, the fucceeding King, by the Earle of *Effex*, untill he was able to fubfift by himfelfe, and till, by her fupport he was ftrengthened, both to overthrow the League, and become a fecond ballance againft the great, and vaft defires of *Spain*.

Neither did fhe reft here, or give him breath, but with a Fleet of one hundred and fifty Sayle, and a ftrong Land-army,
fent

sent the Earl of *Essex*, and the Admirall of *England* to invade *Spaine* it selfe, they tooke *Cales*, spoiled his Fleet of twenty Gallyes, and fifty nine Ships, the riches whereof were valued at twelve millions of Duckets. Immediately after, imployed she not the Earle of *Essex* with a Fleet to the Islands? In which Voyage he sacked *Villa Franca*, and tooke prizes to the value of foure hundred thousand Duckets at the least.

Now when this Spanish Invader found him selfe thus well paid with his owne coyne, and so forced to divert the provoked hand of that famous Queen held over him, by stirring up *Tirone* in *Ireland*; to which end he sent money, and Forces under *Don Iohn d' Aquila*, even then that Lady, first by *Essex*, and after by *Montjoy*, overthrew the Irish, and sent home the Spaniard well recompenced with losse, and dishonour for assisting her Rebels.

By which and the like active courses of hers in successive, and successefull undertakings, that provident Lady both bore out the charge of all those expeditions,

tions, requited his Invafion, clipped the fearfull wings of this growing Monarch, and made his credit fwell through all the mony-banks of Europe, caufing withall as low an Ebbe of his treafure.

Againe by this imprifoning of the Lyon within his owne den, fhe did not only leffen his reputation (a chiefe ftrength of growing Monarchs) but difcovered fuch a light as perchance might have forced him in time, to difpute the Titles of his Ufurpations at home, and have given *Portugall*, *Arragon*, and *Granada* opportunity to plead their rights with *Caftile* in the Courts of *Mars*, if God had either lengthened the dayes of that worthy Lady who underftood him, or time not neglected her wifdome fo fuddenly, by exchanging that active, victorious, enriching, and ballancing courfe of her defenfive Wars, for an idle (I feare) deceiving fhadow of peace. In which whether we already languifh, or live impoverifhed, whilft he growes potent, and rich, by the fatall fecurity of all Chriftendome, they that fhall fucceed us, are like to feele, and judge freely.

Thus

Thus you fee how our famous *Iudith* difperfed the terrour of this *Holofernes*, like a cloud full of wind, and by a Princely wakefulneffe, preferved all thofe Soveraigne States that were in league with her, from the dangerous temptations of power, wealth, and practice, by which the growing Monarchs doe often intangle the inferior, but yet Soveraigne Princes. And amongft the reft, from that ufuall traffique of his Leiger Embaffadors, who trained up in the nimble exchange of Intelligence, grow to be of fuch a *Bucephalus* nature, fo like *Rome*, as I faid before, a body of fuch members, as the *Alexanders* of their time can only mannage, and make ufe of; Inftance *Mendofa*, in whom fhe had long before difcovered, and difcredited all practifes of thofe fpecious imployments of Conquerers Agents.

Befides in honour of her be it fpoken, did not this mirrour of Juftice, by reftraining that unnaturall ambition of getting other Princes rights, within the naturall bounds of well-governing her owne, become a beame of fuch credit, as most of the Kings, or States then raigning, freely yeelded; both to weigh their owne interests within the scales of her judgment, and besides to assist her in bounding out the Imperiall Meeres of all Princes by the ancient procession of Right, and power.

Lastly, did she not purchase the like reputation even amongst the heathen, and by it destroy'd a nest, which this aspiring Monarch began to build in the Seraglio of *Constantinople*; For she thinking it no wisdome to look on, and see his Spanish pistols pierce into so high a mountaine of Forces, and dispose of them at his pleasure, providently opened the stronger Monarchs eyes to discover how craftily the weaker wrought his ends at the cost of all defective, or sleepy Princes about her.

Yet did not this Soveraigne Lady intercept his designes from under any Goddesse shield (whom *Homer* makes the Grecian Worthies shoot, and hit) but displanted him by a gallant Factor of her Merchants in a league of Traffique, and prevailed to make his Embassador landed

landed at *Ragufa*, houfed in *Conftantinople*, and all under protection of *Ferrat* chiefe Vifier, yet, and upon a contract of thirty thoufand zecchins already paid him, glad to returne, and fhippe himfelfe away, with more expedition then he landed.

Befides which reputation given to her name by the Grand Signior in this particular, fhe generally got power to keep this fearfull Standard of the halfe Moon waving in fuch manner over all the King of Spaines defignes, as he durft move no where againft his Neighbour-Chriftian-Princes, for feare of being incompaffed within the horns of the heathen Crefcent.

But thefe things fwell, and require a more authenticall Hiftory, to continue the memory of that wonder of Queens, and women ; in honour of whofe facred name, I have prefumed thus to digreffe, and admonifh all Eftates by her example, how they may draw ufe, and honour, both from the dead, and the living, the change of times having no power over reall wifdomes, but infinite over the
fhadowes

shadowes of craft, and humours of petty States, which commonly follow the greater Bodies, as they are unequally extended, or contracted about them.

Wherefore now to conclude these Heroicall Enterprises abroad, together with the reformations of her State at home, the refining of the English Standard embased by her sister, the preservation of her Crown-Revenue intire, her wisdome in the change of Lawes, without change of dangers, the timely and Princely help she gave to *Henry* the fourth when he had nothing but the Towne of *Diepe* left him, his credit, and meanes being utterly exhausted, and so that brave King ready, either to take Sea, and escape, or flye for succour into *England*, her constant establishment of Religion in *Ireland*, driving the Spanish Forces divers times from thence, who were maliciously sent as well to stirre up her subjects to rebell as to maintaine, and support them in it, together with the former recited particulars, howsoever improperly disperfed, or bundled up together, yet are in their natures of so

rare

rare a wifdome, as I beleeve they will ftill be more and more admired, and juftly, in that excellent Princeffe, even many Ages after her death.

Thus have I by the Readers patience, given that Ægyptian, and Roman Tragedy a much more honourable fepulture, then it could ever have deferved, efpecially in making their memories to attend upon my Soveraignes herfe, without any other hope of being, then to wait upon her life, and death, as their Maker did, who hath ever fince been dying to all thofe glories of Life which he formerly enjoyed, under the bleffed, and bleffing prefence of this unmatchable Queen and woman.

Now if any man fhall demand why I did not rather leave unto the world a complete hiftory of her Life, then this fhort memoriall in fuch fcatter'd, and undifgefted minutes, let him receive this anfwer from a dead man, becaufe I am confident no flefh breathing (by feeing what is done) fhall have occafion of asking that queftion, whileft I am living. Prefently after the death of
my

my moft gracious Queen, and Miftrefs, the falfe fpirits, and apparitions of idle griefe haunted me exceedingly, and made all things feeme either greater, or leffe then they were; fo that the farther I went, the more difcomfortable I found thofe new refolutions of time, to my decayed, and difproportioned abilities; yet fearing to be curfed with the Figg-tree, if I bore no fruit, I rouzed up my thoughts upon an ancient axiome of Wife men; *Si quicquid offendit, relinquimus citò; inerti otio torpebit vita*; and upon a fecond review of the world, called to mind the many duties I ought to that matchleffe Soveraigne of mine, with a refolution to write her life in this manner.

Firft, curioufly to have begun with the uniting of the Red, and White Rofes, in the marriage of *Hen:* the feventh; In the like manner to have run over *Henry* the eighths time, untill his feverall rents in the Church, with a purpofe to have demurr'd more ferioufly upon the fudden change in his Sonne *Edward* the fixth, from fuperftition

tion to the eftablifhment of Gods Ancient, Catholique, and Primitive Church; thofe cobwebs of re-converfion in Queen *Maryes* dayes, I had no intent to meddle with, but only by pre-occupation to fhew, that Princes captived in Nature, can feldome keep any thing free in their Governments, but as foyles manured to bring forth ill weeds apace, muft live to fee Schifme arife in the Church, wearing out the reall branches of immortall truth, to weave in the thin leaves of mortall fuperftition, and to behold in the State all their faireft induftries fpring, and fade together, like Ferne-feed; Laftly, I intended with fuch fpirits, as Age had left me, to revive my felf in her memory, under whom I was bred.

Now in this courfe, becaufe I knew, that as the liberality of Kings did help to cover many errours, fo truth in a ftory would make good many other defects in the writer, I adventured to move the Secretary, that I might have his favour to perufe all obfolete Records of the Councell-cheft, from thofe times downe as near to thefe, as he in

his

his wifdome fhould think fit; hee firft friendly required my end in it, which I as freely delivered him, as I have now done to you.

Againft her memory he, of all men, had no reafon to keep a ftrict hand, and where to beftow a Queen *Elizabeths* fervant with leffe difadvantage to himfelfe it feems readily appeared not; fo that my abrupt motion tooke hold of his prefent Counfell. For he liberally granted my requeft, and appointed me that day three weeks to come for his warrant, which I did, and then found in fhew a more familiar, and gracefull afpect then before, he defcending to queftion me, why I would dreame out my time in writing a ftory, being as like to rife in this time as any man he knew; Then in a more ferious, and friendly manner examining me, how I could cleerly deliver many things done in that time, which might perchance be conftrued to the prejudice of this.

I fhortly made anfwer, that I conceivd an Hiftorian was bound to tell nothing but the truth, but to tell all truths
were

were both juftly to wrong, and offend not only Princes, and States, but to blemifh, and ftir up againft himfelfe, the frailty and tenderneffe, not only of particular men, but of many Families, with the fpirit of an *Athenian Timon*; And therefore fhewed my felfe fo far from being difcouraged with that objection, as I took upon me freely to adventure all my own goods in this Ship, which was to be of my owne building. Immediately this Noble Secretary, as it feems, moved, but not removed with thofe felfeneffes of my opinion, ferioufly affured me, that upon fecond thoughts he durft not prefume to let the Councell-cheft lie open to any man living, without his Majefties knowledge and approbation.

With this fuperfedeas I humbly took my leave, at the firft fight affuring my felfe this laft project of his would neceffarily require fheet after fheet to be viewed, which I had no confidence in my own powers to abide the hazard of; and herein it may pleafe the Reader to beleeve me the rather by thefe
Pamphlets,

Pamphlets, which having flept out my own time, if they happen to be feene hereafter, fhall at their own perill rife upon the ftage, when I am not; Befides, in the fame propofition I further faw, that the many Judgements, which thofe *Embryoes* of mine muft probably have paft through, would have brought forth fuch a world of alterations, as in the end the worke it felfe would have proved a ftory of other mens writing, with my name only to put to it, and fo a worfhip of time, not a voluntary homage of duty.

Farther I cannot juftifie thefe little fparkes, unworthy of her, and unfit for me; fo that I muft conclude with this ingenuous *Confeßion*, that it grieves me to know I fhall (as far as this abrupt Apology extends) live, and dye upon equall tearmes with a Queene, and Creature fo many waies unequall, nay, infinitely fuperiour to me, both in Nature, and Fortune.

*CAP.*

## CAP. XVIII.

Now to return to the Tragedies remaining, my purpose in them was, not (with the Ancient) to exemplifie the disastrous miseries of mans life, where Order, Lawes, Doctrine, and Authority are unable to protect Innocency from the exorbitant wickednesse of power, and so out of that melancholike Vision, stir horrour, or murmur against Divine Providence: nor yet (with the Moderne) to point out Gods revenging aspect upon every particular sin, to the despaire, or confusion of mortality; but rather to trace out the high waies of ambitious Governours, and to shew in the practice, that the more audacity, advantage, and good successe such Soveraignties have, the more they hasten to their owne desolation and ruine.

So that to this abstract end, finding all little instruments in discovery of
great

great bodies to be feldome without errours, I prefumed, or it rather efcaped me, to make my Images beyond the ordinary ftature of exceffe, wherein again that women are predominant, is not for malice, or ill talent to their Sexe; But as Poets figured the vertues to be women, and all Nations call them by Feminine names, fo have I defcribed malice, craft, and fuch like vices in the perfons of Shrews, to fhew that many of them are of that nature, even as we are, I meane ftrong in weakneffe; and confequently in thefe Orbes of Paffion, the weaker Sexe commonly the moft predominant; yet as I have not made all women good with *Euripides*, fo have I not made them all evill with *Sophocles*, but mixt of fuch forts as we find both them, and our felves.

Againe, for the Arguments of thefe Tragedies they be not naked, and cafuall, like the Greeke, and Latine, nor (I confeffe) contrived with the variety, and unexpected encounters of the Italians, but nearer Level'd to thofe humours, councels, and practices, wherein I thought
fitter

fitter to hold the attention of the Reader, than in the ftrangenefs, or perplexednefs of witty Fictions; In which the affections, or imagination, may perchance find exercife, and entertainment, but the memory and judgement no enriching at all; Befides, I conceived thefe delicate Images to be over-abundantly furnilhed in all Languages already.

And though my Noble Friend had that dexterity, even with the dalhes of his pen to make the *Arcadian* Antiques beautifie the Margents of his works; yet the honour which (I beare him record) he never affected, I leave unto him, with this addition, that his end in them was not vanilhing pleafure alone, but morall Images, and Examples, (as directing threds) to guide every man through the confufed *Labyrinth* of his own defires, and life: So that howfoever I liked them too well (even in that unperfected lhape they were) to condefcend that fuch delicate (though inferior) Pictures of himfelfe, fhould be fuppreffed; yet I do wilh that work may be the laft in this kind, prefuming no

man

man that followes can ever reach, much leffe go beyond that excellent intended patterne of his.

For my own part, I found my creeping Genius more fixed upon the Images of Life, than the Images of Wit, and therefore chofe not to write to them on whofe foot the black Oxe had not already trod, as the Proverbe is, but to thofe only, that are weather-beaten in the Sea of this World, fuch as having loft the fight of their Gardens, and groves, ftudy to faile on a right courfe among Rocks, and quick-fands; And if in thus ordaining, and ordering matter, and forme together for the ufe of life, I have made thofe Tragedies, no Plaies for the Stage, be it known, it was no part of my purpofe to write for them, againft whom fo many good, and great fpirits have already written.

But he that will behold thefe Acts upon their true Stage, let him look on that Stage wherein himfelf is an Actor, even the ftate he lives in, and for every part he may perchance find a Player, and for every Line (it may be) an
                    inftance

inftance of life, beyond the Authors intention, or application, the vices of former Ages being fo like to thefe of this Age, as it will be eafie to find out fome affinity, or refemblance between them, which whofoever readeth with this apprehenfion, will not perchance thinke the Scenes too large, at leaft the matter not to be exceeded in account of words.

Laftly, for the Stile; as it is rich, or poore, according to the eftate, and ability of the Writer, fo the value of it fhall be enhanfed, or cried downe, according to the grace, and the capacity of the Reader, from which common Fortune of Bookes, I look for no exemption.

But to conclude, as I began this worke to entertaine, and inftruct my felfe, fo if any other find entertainement, or profit by it, let him ufe it freely, judge honourably of my friend, and moderately of me, which is all the returne that out of this barren Stock can be defired, or expected.

FINIS.

# NOTES

*Title.* The full title was doubtless supplied by the Editor of 1652. In M the heading is merely 'A Dedication to Sʳ Philip Sidney'.

*Epistle Dedicatory.* The Countess of Sunderland was Lady Dorothea Sidney, sister of Algernon Sidney, and the Sacharissa of Waller's poems.

l. 3. well-limb'd = well-limn'd: this spelling occurs occasionally in sixteenth- and seventeenth-century books.

PAGE 2, l. 7 from bot. *Characteristicall,* i.e. (as explained in the following sentence) describing characteristics; in later language 'moral' or 'ethical'.

l. 2 from bot. P misprints 'unfeigned' for 'in feigned'.

5, l. 4. as it were even racked with native strengths] M reads 'ranked', which reading Grosart attributes to P. For 'native strengths' cp. p. 176, l. 5 from bot. The phrase means that her natural qualities of character were, so to speak, too strong for her body—a fanciful way of accounting for her disfigurement by the small-pox.

par. 2, l. 3. ingenious] P sometimes, M usually, writes 'ingenious' where we should now write 'ingenuous'.

6, l. 1. acme M: aim P.

7, l. 6. After 'Arcadia' M inserts 'a Frenchman borne'.

7, l. 13. M reads 'got him light enough'. Languet was born at Viteaux in Burgundy in 1518, took the degree of Doctor of Laws at Padua, became a friend of Melanchthon and a convert to the Reformation, was employed as a diplomatist, especially by Augustus, Elector of Saxony, and died in 1581. The Wechel mentioned in this connexion was Andrew, son of the famous Paris printer, Christopher Wechel. At the time of the massacre of St. Bartholomew Languet was lodging with Wechel in Paris, and managed to protect him as well as de Mornay, the friend of Henry of Navarre. Wechel moved the next year to Frankfort, where his press became as famous as his father's had been at Paris.

9, l. 5. hache (i.e. hatch) M: hath P.

l. 15. be P: lye M. These letters were first published, long after Greville wrote this passage, in 1632.

l. 18. *salves* means both 'greetings' and (as opposed to 'real and large complexions') 'made-up complexions', 'patches', a not uncommon use in the sixteenth and seventeenth centuries. Cp. Bishop Hall (1608), *Char. Virtues and V.* ii. 117, 'He hath salves for every sore . . . complexion for every face.' Hall here uses 'complexion' in the sense of artificial colouring. Greville uses it primarily in the old meaning of 'temperament', 'disposition', but with an eye to its modern meaning, which was only beginning in the seventeenth century to oust the old one. See *N.E.D.* I think Greville is playing on both the words 'complexions' and 'salves'; he is fond of this sarcastic kind of pun.

10, l. 9. Grosart reports both M and P as reading

# Notes

ing 'omnious', which he apparently takes as a genuine variant for 'ominous'. Only P reads 'omnious', evidently a misprint.

10, par. 2, l. 9. chance M: change P. Below, p. 13, par. 2, l. 1, M is in error, reading 'changable for 'chanceable'.

11, par. 2, l. 4. his M: this P.

l. 6. Romanties P: Romantiae M.

l. 7. foure-eyd P: a misprint for 'soure-eyd': sower-eyed M.

l. 12. wonder M: wander P.

12, l. 2. Grosart notes wrongly 'P, puts comma after faith instead of after second-hand'. The fact is that M has comma after 'second-hand' and after 'faith'. P reads as in the text.

13, l. 7. M omits 'home-born'.

16, l. 12. smilings M: smiling P.

17, l. 3. this P: his M, perhaps rightly.

l. 4 from bot. ingenuous P: ingenious M, but meaning the same thing, i. e. worthy of a free-born man.

l. 2 from bot. treits M: tracts P.

18, l. 8. P has a semicolon after 'himself', which obscures the sense more even than the many superfluous commas of that age.

par. 2, l. 2. commanding M: commending P.

l. 4 from bot. P omits 'looke'. sunn M: same P. Grosart prints 'same', which makes no sense, without noticing the correct reading of M.

19, l. 4 from bot. M inserts 'I say' after 'seemes'.

20, l. 8. I insert a comma after 'reservedness', to make the sense clear at first sight.

l. 9. Grosart omits 'with' without comment, presumably by accident: the word is in M and P.

20, l. 2 from bot. P. has, by misprint, 'deservedness.'

21, end of par. 1. I have removed the comma after the first 'Prince', finding by experience that the sense was easily missed. A modern writer would probably write 'no-Prince'.

23, l. 9. to M : by P, Grosart, who does not notice M's reading.

24, l. 15. an Agent] This was William Harborne, who, after visiting Turkey in 1577 and procuring an offer of friendship from the Grand Signior, was appointed the first Envoy or Agent of Elizabeth at Constantinople in 1582. Accounts of his journeys to and from Turkey are given in Hakluyt's Collection. This sentence is characteristically involved. 'Into whose' is governed by 'infusing': 'charge,' as elsewhere, ='expenditure of money or labour'.

25, l. 3 from bot. *Fess*=Fez.

27, par. 2, l. 2. Grosart prints 'comandments', not observing the sign of abbreviation.

l. 2 from bot. M reads 'did not, or could not value it so high'.

28, l. 7. P has the catchword 'in-' at the bottom of p. 32, but accidentally omits 'interest' at the top of p. 33.

29, l. 6. ever P : ouer M.
    par. 2, l. 4. M omits 'own'.
    par. 2, l. 9. over P : upon M.
    bot. M omits 'record'.

30, par. 2, l. 2. M omits 'gladly'.

32, l. 4. M punctuates 'as by descent, to a youth; of grace, as to a stranger',—which keeps the meaning clear. Grosart punctuates 'as by descent, to a youth of grace as to a stranger',—which

## Notes 231

which makes no sense. The meaning is that Don John of Austria showed Sidney condescension as to a youth, grace as to a stranger, and especial punctiliousness in the interchange of courtesies as to an enemy.

    32, l. 9. M misreads 'his' for 'this'. This mistake, which Grosart notices, might have made him pause in his earlier preferences of M's 'his' to P's 'this'. It is evident that the archetype from which both M and P are derived wrote 'his' and 'this' very much alike. On the whole perhaps M is more often right than P in this word.

    par. 2, l. 5. against P: amongst M, Grosart.

    33, par. 2, l. 11. Maecenas M: Mecaenas P, Grosart.

    34, par. 2, l. 7. humorous=wayward.

    par. 2, l. 9. reverend=reverent. M inserts 'kinde of' between 'reverend' and 'ambition'.

    37, l. 12. his M: this P.

    14 foll. One of Greville's obscurer passages. I think it may be paraphrased thus:—' Experience has shown that it has been the usual habit or "school" of greatness to be tender of itself only, making honour a triumph, or rather trophy of desire, set up in the eyes of mankind, to the end that great men either are worshipped as idols, or, as rebels against constituted authority, perish under the compulsion to follow glory which she (Greatness) lays upon them.' That is, Greatness is a selfish tyrant over its victims, great men. The great man worshipped as an idol, and the great man falling as a rebel, were objects always striking, but more familiar to England of Tudor times than at later periods. For the language we may compare the *Inquisition upon Fame and Honour*, e.g. stanza 71 :—

    Lastly,

Lastly, this fame hard gotten, worse to keep,
Is never lost but with despaire and shame;
Which makes man's nature, once fallen from
    this steepe,
Disdaine their being should out-last their name:
Some in selfe-pitty, some in exile languish,
Others rebell, some kill themselves in anguish—

and stanza 86:—

Who worship Fame, commit idolatry,
Make men their God, Fortune and Time their
    worth;
Forme but reforme not—meer hypocrisie!—
By shadowes, onely shadowes bringing forth,
  Which must, as blossomes, fade ere true fruit
    springs;
    —Like voice and eccho—joyn'd yet divers
    things.

39, l. 7. This rather oddly expressed description of Lysander refers to the fact, emphasized by Plutarch, that Lysander was himself superior to the temptation of avarice, but that he corrupted the Spartans by introducing so much gold and silver as the spoils of his conquests and presents of foreign rulers. The allusion to Themistocles is not so easy to explain. Plutarch expressly states that Themistocles was an impartial judge.

l. 5 from bot. I may well say P: may we truely say M.

40, l. 3. censured = estimated.
l. 6. seemed P: loomed M.
l. 15. 'been' here has to do duty for some such phrase as 'resulted in'. If Sidney had found himself inferior to any one in dignity or position, he would have treated such an one with humble obedience,

obedience, even if the man had been a petty Sicilian tyrant.

41, l. 7. P wrongly inserts 'but' before 'such'.

l. 3 from bot. The printer of P after 'service to' at the bottom of p. 48 went on at the top of p. 49 'the Empire? For under', &c., his eye catching the end of the previous sentence, so that the words from 'the Empire' to 'service to' occur twice over. The erratic character of seventeenth-century printing is illustrated by the fact that in the first version he prints 'shaddow', 'Did,' 'reall,' in the second 'shadow', 'did,' 'real.'

l. 2 from bot. an P : one M, Grosart.

42, l. 2 from bot. this M, Grosart: their P. I have taken 'this' as it makes the sense clearer. The conjunction is that of Rome and Spain, whereas 'their' at first reading suggests the German Princes.

43, l. 14. finely P: finally M, Grosart. 'Finally' is perhaps right, but I give the *lectio exquisitior* as it has possession of the text.

44, l. 9. symbolize=form a league for mutual protection, a sense which, as far as I know, Greville derived from the Greek.

par. 2, l. 6. support M: suport P, by a misprint which Grosart does not notice. Just above, Grosart, presumably by a misprint, reports P as reading 'contines' for 'continues'.

45, end of ch. 4. prize which did enfranchise this Master Spirit,&c.] 'Master-prize' or 'master's-prize' occurs fairly often in seventeenth-century literature, especially drama, in one sense of 'master-piece', viz. a piece of work done by an apprentice in order to qualify as a master worker.

On

On p. 49, l. 4, 'master prize'='master-piece' in its more usual signification.

46, l. 13. Poetical=fictitious. Cp. p. 50, l. 2.

47, l. 12. Philip II defeated the French at St. Quintin in 1557, having drawn England into declaring war on France. Greville means that this victory was no more profitable to England than the loss of Calais in the following year.

48, l. 12. Cp. p. 58, end of par. 1.

49, l. 4. M (Grosart wrongly says P) drops 'his' before 'playing'. For 'master prize'= 'master-piece' see note on p. 45, end of ch. iv, above.

par. 2, l. 3. curious P: enuiouse M, Grosart, perhaps rightly.

50, l. 4. Dolman was the fictitious publisher's name under which the famous Jesuit Father Parsons brought out his anonymous *Conference about the next Succession to the Crowne of Ingland* (1594). The authorship seems to have been known to many, but as late as 1603 Sir Anthony Standen in a letter to Parsons himself (*Calendar of State Papers Domestic* 1603, Addenda p. 435) speaks of 'Dolman's book' as if the treatise went by that name, and Greville here writing still later seems not to be aware that Dolman was a man of straw.

par. 2, l. 7. sect P: sorte M. Grosart calls 'sect' a gross misreading, but it is clearly the better word here. For the use of 'sect' cp. p. 54, l. 9 from bot.

l. 4 from bot. under ... Covert Baron = under the guardianship of a husband.

51, l. 2. P omits 'an', which I restore from M.

l. 6. M misreads 'minds' for 'mines', as Grosart notices.

51, l. 5 from bot. Grosart follows M in reading 'the holy mother the Church': but P is surely right in omitting the second 'the'. 'The holy mother church' is the Roman Church, so styled in the thought of the supposed Roman Catholic Consort of Queen Elizabeth. Cp. pp. 58, l. 6; 75, l. 6 from bot. The whole paragraph means that the Duke of Anjou, if he had become Elizabeth's husband, would have tried to change the religion of England thirdly by stretching points of doctrine so as to bring Anglican views nearer to Roman; so making men's minds waver, and gradually seeing how far he could go, not by open toleration of Roman doctrines and practices, but by conniving at them—such connivance being a snare, i.e. being able to be disavowed or not, according to the convenience of the ruling power.

52, l. 4. conference = conversation.

l. 9 from bot. earth-eyd M, Grosart: earth-cy P. P's reading is clearly a mistake: but the expression 'earth-eyd' is difficult. I suppose it means that our common law works underground, like a mole, no one exactly knowing which direction it is taking; and so it lends itself to the use of the sovereign without his 'absoluteness' being open and openly resisted.

53, l. 7. sheer=shear, fleece.

l. 8. bondage P, Grosart: pondage M, which Grosart reports as 'poundage'.

l. 12. This is textually one of the most important passages. M omits 'Danaus' and leaves a space, the copyist evidently being unable to read his original or to supply the word by conjecture. M also omits all the words from 'of prodigality' to 'old age', inclusive, thereby reducing the passage

sage to nonsense. The thought is in itself subtle : by taxing the people for merely wasteful expenditure to bolster up tyranny, because the people will be too impoverished to rise against it. It is, however, inconsistent with the seventh device which follows.

53, last l. under the envy of that art = under the odium attaching to the 'multitude of impoverishing impositions'. The reference to the Duc de Guise alludes to his leadership of the League and dictation of his will to Henry III of France (1585-8).

54, l. 8. P misprints 'Garmany'.

l. 11. Religion, and traffique M, Grosart: Religion, suffique P, by mistake.

l. 4 from bot. 'and' would be more correct than 'or', in which however P and M agree

55, l. 5 from bot. Grosart wrongly attributes M's false reading 'constrain'd' to P.

56, l. 4. money P: men M, Grosart. 'Money' suits 'much' better, and 'men' is tautologous with 'bloud'.

l. 9. M omits 'reciprocally'.

l. 6 from bot. Want of understanding is shown in M here, which reads 'misteries; a multiplie native wealth by improveing their manhood at home', &c., and just below 'defects as (he said)'. Grosart gives no idea of this state of M's text.

57, l. 7. or M, Grosart: in P, by misprint owing to 'invasion' following.

l. 12. A stronger stop at 'them' would make the construction clearer: 'dangerous neighbours,' 'prejudice,' 'a terror,' 'apt,' all being predicates after 'make them become'.

57, last line.

57, last line. costrain P, by misprint: cp. p. 58, last line, where it prints 'constraining'.

59, l. 4. Scirpalus was the pirate who captured Diogenes the Cynic and sold him in Crete: Diog. Laert. 6. 74. Grosart has the wonderful note: 'Qy = Sarpedon cf. *Iliad* vi. 199; ii. 876; v. 479 &c. &c.'    annoy M: among P.

l. 8 from bot. The sense would be more easily caught with a comma at 'universally' and a semicolon at 'spoil'.

62, par. 2, l. 12. Greville is perhaps referring to that part of the story of Lamia which relates that, when she became, through Hera's jealousy, a disfigured childless fury, Zeus gave her the power of taking her eyes out of her head and putting them in again (cp. *Dict. of Myth.*). Sidney would have found that the courtiers only looked at Worth, Justice, and Duty when it suited them. Or he may mean merely that they looked with the distorted eyes of rage at qualities which they did not possess, just as Lamia, robbed of her own children, looked at other people's.

par. 2, l. 13. stained=obscured, kept from the Queen's favour, disgraced; cp. Shakespeare, *Sonnets*, xxxv (quoted in *Century Dict.*), 'Clouds and eclipses stain both moon and sun.'

63, l. 12. born P: bound M, Grosart.

64, l. 13. Grosart adopts M's reading 'passion, swoln with the windes of this'. But 'his' is clearly right. It means that the Earl of Oxford's party was at this time in power. Oxford's wife was a daughter of Lord Burghley.

65, l. 16. M inserts 'an' before 'inward', perhaps rightly.

66, l. 13. to P: of M, perhaps rightly.

66, l. 7

66, l. 7 from bot. P and M agree in 'humours', and the word is freely used by Greville as by other sixteenth- and seventeenth-century writers in various senses that can be derived from the old physiological theory of the 'cardinal humours' or fluids of the body, the mixture of which in various proportions was the cause of the varieties of human character. Still 'honour' is a tempting emendation here.

69, l. 8 from bot. president=precedent: so too p. 173, par. 3, l. 8.

71, l. 3. This use of 'dispense with'='put up with, allow' (the opposite of the more usual meaning 'do without, remit') is first quoted in *N.E.D.* from Sidney himself. It occurs occasionally in seventeenth- and eighteenth-century writers.

72, l. 3 from bot. for M: from P, wrongly. Grosart says 'stupidly', but applies no epithet to M's omission of 'more' before 'secret' in the middle of the previous paragraph, or substitution of 'with' for 'without' at the end of the same.

73, l. 8. industrous P: industrious M. Both forms are found in sixteenth- and seventeenth-century writers: cp. *N.E.D.*

l. 14. Don Antonio was the pretender to the throne of Portugal in support of whose claims Elizabeth authorized the unsuccessful expedition of Sir John Norreys and Francis Drake in 1589.

75, l. 1. M inserts 'but' before 'it may be', and it improves the sentence. Grosart reports M as reading 'bot'. I think the word is meant for 'but'; but it is written so small that the ink has filled up the curve of the 'u'.

par. 2, l. 6. his M: this P.

l. 5 from bot. Grosart reads 'fit' with note 'Query—

'Query—sit?' But both M and P read 'sit', M in the form 'sitte'.

76, l. 5. although P: as though M, Grosart, who absurdly says 'P grossly misprints "although"'. 'Although' makes sense, 'as though' none.

l. 10. I have here ventured on an emendation which is, I think, certain: viz. 'selfnesses' for 'salfe places' of P, 'sealf places' of M. (Grosart misreports P as misreading 'false'). 'Selfness' is a word characteristic of Greville: for the plural cp. p. 114 last line: and for the antithesis with the duty of obedience, p. 147 at the top.

77, par. 2, end. After 'honor' M has, without any sign of afterthought, the following sentence: 'Yet to deale trulie with the dead, he was a man not only sufficient in the triviall parts of Navigation, but even large beyond his profession in undertakinge that vast Empire of Spaine, a masse so far above him in Councel, wealth, and disciplin'd armies.' ('Undertakinge' is spelled 'untertakinge' by a slip in M). For this and similar serious discrepancies between M and P see the Introduction.

l. 2 from bot. We should probably read 'adventurers'.

78, l. 4. possibilitie M: impossibility P, Grosart, without comment. I had conjectured 'possibility' before finding it in M.

last line. These fine words are used by Wordsworth in a well-known sonnet, *Another year!— another deadly blow!* ll. 12-14:—

A venal Band
Who are to judge of danger which they fear,
And honour which they do not understand.

'These two lines,' says Wordsworth in his note,
'from

'from Lord Brooke's Life of Sir Philip Sydney': a note which first sent me, many years ago, to this treatise.

79, l. 11. M inserts 'in either' after 'govern'd': i.e. 'in either peace or war'.

l. 14. complexions=characters.

l. 5 from bot. creation = nature.

last line. Grosart follows M in wrongly omitting 'she' before 'shewed'.

80, l. 6 from bot. his M: this P.

81, l. 7. prone P: proud M, Grosart. I think P is right. The meaning is that the nobles were restless and turbulent; hence the tendency 'to be cantonized by self-division'.

par. 2. Grosart makes nonsense of this paragraph by following M in reading 'his' before 'false assumpsit'. The sense is obscurely expressed at the best. The paragraph means: He saw the States of the Empire resting upon the Empire's own greatness, and, under this false assumption, giving the rein to the Emperor to do what he liked with them. Cp. p. 25, l. 6.

82, l. 3. M and P agree in the phrase 'of serving humanity': the only meaning I can read in the words is 'fine schools of which the ostensible purpose was to do service to humane learning'; but the expression is not satisfactory.

par. 2, l. 1. The like mist these craftie mist-raisers intented M: The like mist these crafty-raisers invented P. Grosart reads, as if from M, 'The like craftie mist-raisers intented,' making nonsense. 'Intented'='intended', and is so used as late as Greville (e.g. Holinshed 1577–87: *N.E.D.*): perhaps the obsolete form led to P's mistaken 'invented'.

83, l. 7.

## Notes

83, l. 7. their P: his M, Grosart. 'His' may be right and would be more grammatical, referring to the 'Monarchie of Spain': but at the beginning of the next paragraph Greville takes up the same subject with 'they'; and in fact he has in his mind, as usual, the composite subject, the arch-enemy of the Reformed Churches, Spain and Rome combined.

par. 2, l. 4 from bot. enticements M (not noticed by Grosart): exticements P, Grosart (a *vox nihili*, for which Sir Egerton Brydges substituted 'excitements').

84, par. 3, l. 3. Polack M: Polae P.

l. 7. The sentence 'The King . . . active Princes' is omitted by M.

l. 3 from bot. M inserts 'kept' before 'quiet', and is probably right: this and the two previous clauses, though punctuated as independent sentences, are in sense subordinate to and explanatory of the first clause of the paragraph.

85, par. 2, l. 3. not P: most M, Grosart.

par. 3, l. 4. force P: feare M, very likely rightly.

l. 5 from bot. 'challenging their own' apparently means 'asserting their own rights'.

86, l. 6 from bot. voices P: vices M, Grosart, making no sense. Greville means that Spain had Cardinals in her pay who voted in her interest in the Conclave.

87, par. 2, l. 1. P inserts 'And' before 'out of which', and Grosart here strangely deserts M, which rightly omits it.

88, l. 6 from bot. could P: would M.

89, par. 2 at end. After 'discipline': M adds 'and so like the manie passages of a medicine, loose

loose a great part of their vertue, before they come to worke'.
    89, par. 3, l. 1. And so P: Whereupon he M.
l. 6 from bot. cp. Caesar, *Bell. Gall.* iv. 5.
    90, l. 7 from bot. all havens P: every haven M. M writes 'the' by mistake for 'they'.
    91, l. 6. M omits 'if . . . monies'.
    l. 2 from bot. 'this reall inquisition' seems to mean this inquisition into the power of Spain and the possibilities of overthrowing that power, as contrasted, by a sort of pun, with the Spanish Inquisition. But it is perhaps worth notice that on p. 93, l. 5 from bot. we have the expression 'Regall inquisition'.
    92, l. 9. Cales=Cadiz, as p. 172, l. 5 from bot. The form 'Cales' was in common use in the sixteenth century. Thus in Minsheu's *Spanish-English Dict.* (1599) we have 'Cádis: the city of Cales in Spain'. On the other hand in Stevens's *Dict.* (1706) in a fairly long article on Cadiz there is no mention of the form 'Cales'. Zedler's *Universal Lexicon* recognizes the forms 'Cadis, Cadix, oder Calis'. For the danger of confusion with Calais cp. note on p. 97, l. 6 from bot.
    l. 8 from bot. bin P: layne (corrected from layd) M.
    93, l. 7. I have corrected P's 'commodius'. M writes 'comodiouse'.
    l. 12. M omits 'I mean'.
    94, par. 2, ll. 6, 7. Both P and M read 'sex' and 'sexes' here, but it is obvious that Greville is referring to religious 'sects'. 'All sexes,' moreover, in the usual sense of 'sex', is an expression devoid of meaning. It seems possible that Greville is employing a sort of pun, especially as in his day
'sect'

'sect' was sometimes used for 'sex', as in Shakespeare, *II Henry the Fourth*, ii. 4. 41 : 'So is all her sect; an they be once in a calm, they are sick.' The serious meaning of the passage, however, seems clearly to be that Queen Elizabeth rested with her sects at home (i.e. did not unnecessarily stir up religious strife in England) but moved all sects abroad (i.e. stirred up the Huguenots, the Lutherans, &c., in her active foreign policy).

95, l. 5. Domanies P, by misprint: demeasnes M.

par. 2, l. 3. divisions M: diversions P.

l. 9. disorder M: *Discorder* P, Grosart, without comment. This passage is, curiously, quoted in *N.E.D.* as an instance of the word 'Discorder', together with a single instance of 'dyscordour' ('a stryver, a dyscordour') *c.* 1400 A.D. Before seeing M I felt sure that Greville wrote either 'Discordia' or 'Disorder'. 'Discorder,' even if it existed, would make no sense here.

96, l. 1. oversoaring M: over-soring P, Grosart.

l. 3. P omits 'it' by mistake.

l. 4. greatest P: great M, which seems the better reading.

l. 5. waving] Cp. p. 204, l. 2 from bot.

l. 9. interruption P: interruptinge M.

l. 12. Roan=Rouen.

97, l. 6. rest P: rests M, Grosart.

par. 1, l. 2 from bot. Grosart says that M omits the 'of' before 'enjoying': but it is really the 'of' before 'over-griping' which M omits, a more venial error.

par. 2, l. 2. *Calice* M: *Cales* P, Grosart, without comment. M is obviously right here. Greville uses the forms 'Calice' (p. 47, l. 13) and 'Callice'

'Callice' (p. 166, l. 10; p. 167, l. 14) for Calais. Cales, as we have seen (note on p. 92, l. 9), is Cadiz.

97, l. 4 from bot. that Mayn P : the maine M. The words 'offered . . . protection' are omitted by M.  P prints a comma after 'offered'.

l. 3 from bot. M inserts 'an' before 'honor' (as it spells 'honour').

98, l. 13. Magistracy into Sale works] This curious expression, if correct, must mean that magistracy had been transformed into a system of buying and selling lucrative offices.

99, l. 2. unsubdued M : subdued P.  P has no stop after 'Germany'; M rightly has.

l. 12. Citadellize = keep in subjection by means of garrisons; cp. p. 56, l. 1.

l. 6 from bot. resolve M : resist P.  M omits 'to'.

100, l. 1. treadinge M : trading P.

l. 4. or P : and M, probably rightly.

l. 7 from bot. Grosart prints 'divisions' without comment.

101, l. 3. &c., and M: P in some copies reads 'and &c.', in others '&c.' alone.  Similarly in some copies P has no comma after 'Navarre'; and in some copies misprints 'intterrupt'; while in others it has neither of these mistakes, thus proving that more than one impression was issued, though without the statement of any new edition.

l. 5. prosecutions P : prosecution M.

l. 6. M omits 'to the same end'.

l. 7. this M : his P.

par. 2, l. 3. more than charge=beyond the expense.

l. 8. M omits 'new', and transposes 'undertaken' and 'league'.

102, l. 3.

102, l. 3. whom P: which M.
  par. 2, l. 12. Powers P: Princes M.
  l. 13. mean P: weake M.
103, l. 4. P has a semicolon after 'weak : M rightly only a comma.
  l. 9. in P: to M.
  l. 11. M omits 'by that course'.
  l. 9 from bot. M inserts 'the' before 'less', probably rightly.
  l. 7 from bot. P in some copies has a comma after 'gallies', in one (at least) a colon.
  l. 3 from bot. P has a comma after instead of before 'rather'.
  l. 2 from bot. or P: not M. M's reading is certainly more pointed and may be right.
104, par. 2, l. 12. P in some copies spells 'Manumissions' correctly, in one (at least) omits the 'u'.
  l. 13. those M: these P.    oppressing P: suppressing M.
  l. 7 from bot. M (Grosart wrongly says P) omits the second 'Spanish'.
  l. 5 from bot. After 'Nation' M inserts 'and their native Princes'.
105, l. 4. M inserts 'nay' before 'even'. The sentence is hardly grammatical, though the sense is plain.
  par. 2, l. 2. would P: could M.
  par. 2, l. 4. M omits 'the'.    'to keep his becoming Chaplain . . .' means 'in order to keep his becoming subject to, a mere Chaplain to, Spain . . .'; cp. p. 58, l. 14.
  par. 2, l. 8. this M: his P.
  l. 2 from bot. whereby he might so preserve P: seeing the Pope thereby might preserve M.
                                                This

This passage is all very obscure, even for this part of the treatise. By substituting a full stop for a comma before 'whereby' (cp. p. 106, l. 6), we get some light on the meaning, since the 'he' of the last line of the page is certainly the Pope. I subjoin a paraphrase of the paragraph. 'Lastly he asked whether the Pope would not, like a man holy but yet of this world, in order to put off his subjection to Spain, connive at, or at any rate not excommunicate, or start a Crusade against, these qualifying Armies, and do this [connive, &c.] merely to moderate the over-greatness of the Spanish monarchy—a monarchy which was nursed under the Papacy and its intrigues, but which now imperiously announces its resolution of abolishing all distinctions among men except that absolute rule of the superiority of the wise and the strong. Acting in this way the Pope might keep his spiritual supremacy, without the religion or the sovereignty of various courts being disturbed (i. e. without pushing the enemies of Spain into utter opposition to the Roman Church and causing wars of religion), and might restore the autonomy of the Italian States. Granted that this would mean that the Pope gave up some of his temporal advantages and the jurisdiction he exercised as the subordinate of Spain; yet still he would increase his spiritual prestige, and with the aid of the other princes shake off the tyranny of Spain.' The latter part of the paragraph is easy enough. For the expression 'qualifying Armies', viz. armies of which the object was to reduce the absoluteness of Spain, cp. p. 107, par. 2, l. 5. For 'that Canonical regiment of wit and might', if I have explained it rightly, cp. Wordsworth, *Rob Roy's Grave*, l. 37:—

'For

For why?—because the good old rule
Sufficeth them, the simple plan,
That they should take, who have the power,
And they should keep, who can.

And, still more closely parallel, though less familiar, line 49:—

All kinds and creatures stand and fall
By strength of prowess or of wit:
'Tis God's appointment who must sway,
And who is to submit.

106, l. 5. free P: freed M, by a slip, which Grosart adopts.
l. 6. M omits 'Whereby'.
l. 10. M omits '(as I said)'.
l. 3 from bot. *Ottoman* P: Augustus M. A most curious variation of reading, which perhaps should be traced to an alteration made by Greville himself or an alternative left undecided. The superficial connexion of Antony and Augustus is obvious; but 'Ottoman' suits the context better than 'Augustus'. It is noticeable that Philip is compared to Augustus in the next paragraph (p. 108, l. 11), but in a more appropriate context. It is possible to imagine Brutus or even Cicero speaking of undertaking Antony separately in order to overthrow the designs of Octavian (whom Greville might speak of as Augustus by a common anachronism), but I know of no definite source for such an allusion. At the same time the reference to Antony by himself is obscure. Possibly, if Greville had not destroyed his tragedy of *Antony and Cleopatra*, we should have found a key to the riddle there. For the phrase 'Spanish Ottoman' cp.

# 248  Notes

cp. p. 99, l. 4 from bottom: 'this devouring *Sultan*.'

107, par. 2, l. 5. those M: these P.
  l. 8 from bot. Nown-adjective-natured] For this quaint but easily understood epithet cp. p. 143, par. 2, l. 6; p. 166, l. 5 from bottom.

108, l. 1. This passage is made hopelessly obscure, no doubt, by the loss of a verb. The sense is that she had seen Philip 'entice' Henry III (or some such expression), just as Spain was now trying to entice the noun-adjective-natured German Princes.
  l. 3. M omits 'fellow-'.
  l. 5. P. misprints 'Amiers'.
  l. 8. Paris P: Roan M. This is a curious variant, because either reading gives equally good sense. In 1590 Alexander Farnese, Duke of Parma, marched from the Netherlands and relieved Paris from the siege of Henry of Navarre; in 1592 he did exactly the same for Rouen: and as both these incidents took place some years after Sir Philip Sidney's death (1586), Greville is in either case combining Sidney's view of politics with later experiences of Elizabeth. It seems not improbable that Greville wrote first one of these towns down and then the other, possibly intending to mention both, possibly forgetting to delete one. I have substituted a full stop after 'Paris' for the comma of P, to save the sense.
  l. 11. *Augustus*-like: referring to Augustus' injunctions to Tiberius not to extend the boundaries of the Empire after his death.
  ll. 13 foll. This sentence loses itself in its tail. The sense is: 'foreseeing that succeeding Princes, with their various characters and dispositions, would

would be unable to maintain such new, unassimilated usurpations (as Amiens, Abbeville, &c.) in the heart of a kingdom which was a rival with his own.' He expands the notion 'his own kingdom' into 'his seven-headed Hydra, which was only kept together by Fortune keeping her wheel in a position favourable to Spain for an unnaturally long time, which would come to an end when some new child of Fortune should come to the top—as did in fact happen when Henry IV came to the throne of France'.

108, l. 7 from bot. restoring = putting back to their former condition, i. e. here 'rectifying'.

l. 3 from bot. these P: those M. I keep 'these' here, as in l. 10 above, where there is no variant. Either word makes equally good sense.

last line. or M: as P, Grosart without noticing the variant. Smoaks = exhalations of a sacrifice: cp. Shakespeare, *Cymbeline*, v. 5. 477:—

Laud we the Gods;
And let our crooked smokes climb to their nostrils
From our blest altars.

109, l. 1. of a dyeinge diseased M: dying of a diseased P, without sense.

l. 5. encrochments M: enchrochments P, Grosart. P spells the word rightly on the previous page.

l. 8. After 'doth' we must supply 'carry'.

par. 2, l. 4. P has dropped the comma after 'left', and the first 'i' of 'inhabite' in l. 6.

l. 6 from bot. The semicolon after 'weakest' is characteristic; the sense would be clearer to us with a comma or even no stop.

110, l. 5. neutralitie M: naturality P.

110, l. 12.

110, l. 12. Grosart reads 'only' before 'grounds', from an obvious mistake of P, in which ' only' is the catchword on p. 123 but is not in the text at the top of p. 124. It has been printed as the catchword by accidental reference to ' only' at the beginning of the next line but two. Grosart solemnly records that M omits it.

l. 5 from bot. Mayne M: Mine P. Cp. p. 117, par. 2, l. 7.

111, par. 2, l. 7. *Cimerons* P. M has a collection of letters evidently written by some one who did not know the word intended. The scribe has tried to imitate the letters of the original and was apparently uncertain whether the 'C' was followed by 'i' or 'm': the result is 'C in n r o ns' or 'C m n r o ns'. The word is more correctly spelt 'Cimarrons', and means (1) wild, uncivilized, (2) runaway negroes, or, as here, natives of the West Indies. Grosart in his text has ' Cinnons', and attributes to P the reading ' Cimenons'.

112, par. 2, l. 2. M omits 'the' wrongly, and is followed by Grosart.

l. 3. conjunction P: comixion M, which Grosart reports as ' commixion '; but there is no sign of doubling over the ' m '. P repeats ' of ' twice before ' Scotland ' and omits it before ' England '.

l. 7. M adds ' of ' after ' disposed ', and omits ' any ' before ' strength '.

113, par. 2, l. 2. over-racked unitie M: racked vanity P. Either expression ' over-stretched unification, or absorption of others into the empire of Spain ', or ' strained, exaggerated, vanity, or vain ambition ', makes good sense, and is consonant with Greville's diction; but (1) it is much more likely that ' over ' has dropped out in P or

its

## Notes

its original than that it has been wrongly inserted in M; (2) 'vanity' is not exactly the word we should expect, but rather 'ambition' or, as on p. 115, par. 2, l. 2, 'bloudy pride,' if this was Greville's meaning, whereas the attempt of Spain to establish an unnatural (over-strained) universal empire is the principal theme of these reflections.

114, l. 9. M has 'against' corrected to 'besides'.
 l. 10. M omits 'Spain' and writes 'barraine' (as on p. 115, l. 12), and omits 'more' in l. 11.
 l. 12. affectations M : affections P.
 l. 15. For the semicolon cp. note on p. 109, l. 6 from bot.
 l. 17, rest P : be M, Grosart.
 l. 3 from bot. laws P : lawe M.
 last line. P misprints 'selfsnesses'.

115, l. 1. over M : other P, by mistake. The construction of the sentence is not clear. It probably means: 'to imprison divine laws within the narrowness of will and of human wisdom, owing to the fettered self-seeking of cowardly or over-confident Tyranny.' But there is a confusion of images, both divine laws and the self-interest of Tyranny being represented as in bondage.

 l. 3. commotion P : comiction M. It is not easy to choose. With 'commotion' the sense is that by restraining the importation of arms Spain keeps its colonies quiet : with 'commiction ', i. e. intercourse, that Spain allows no commerce between her colonies and other countries, as we heard on p. 113, par. 2.

 l. 5. that continually P : out of those desperate councells of oppression M.
 l. 6. free-denized in P : in free-denizend in M:

M: in free denized Grosart, who simply (and wrongly) comments 'P, omits "in"'.
115, l. 14. rack M: rock P. The antithesis to 'ease' makes 'rack' probable, especially as it is a favourite word : otherwise the 'waving' designs of an 'unsteddy' power would favour 'rock'. An unsteady pyramid is a somewhat self-contradictory figure, but Greville is thinking of Spain as perched on the sharp point of the pyramid.

l. 4 from bot. This means that Spain employed the Inquisition not, as formerly, with the pretended purpose of pruning or governing, i. e. of keeping men's religious beliefs under some sort of discipline, but, in a senile over-confidence, with the undisguised purpose of rooting out all freedom of thought. The use of 'masks'='disguised proceedings' is a Grevillian extension of the familiar sense, which seems, however, to have only lately come into use, 'disguise.'

117, l. 5. devily characters P: liuelie chararts M: liuelie characts Grosart, who says 'P, oddly misreads "devily"'. The choice between 'characters' and 'characts' is indifferent; both mean 'features', 'traits,' and Greville uses both (one of the instances referred to by Grosart for 'characts' gives 'character' in the sense 'impression', 'reproduction,' *Caelica*, Sonnet iii, l. 8). As between 'devily' and 'lively', 'devily' gives an excellent antithesis between the 'deity' of the Christians and the 'devilish features' which Spanish barbarity displayed : but it is noticeable that the latest example of this form of the adjective given by N.E.D. (except the passage under discussion) is *circa* 1485. The fact that we have 'lively Images of the dark Prince' just above, p. 116, l. 16, makes 'lively' a plausible a plausible reading, but for that very reason may have led to its substitution for 'devily'. On the whole, I keep P's reading, with diffidence.

117, l. 6 from bot. by that means P: resolued M.

l. 4 from bot. M inserts 'in the South Sea' after 'Fleet'.

118, l. 3 from bot. *Ramas* = heap, collection; cp. French *ramasser*.

119, l. 6. wide the door P: the wide door M.

l. 14. M omits 'mother'.

l. 15. ingenuously P: ingeniouslie M. The two forms are interchangeable in early writers. Here the meaning is nearer our 'ingeniously': more often it is nearer our 'ingenuously', as on the next page, par. 2, l. 7.

120, l. 1. M omits 'the'.

l. 4. undertaker M: undertakers P.

l. 2 from bot. M omits 'to'.

121, par. 2, l. 5. secure P: seuere M, perhaps rightly.

l. 5 from bot. Grosart attributes to P the mistake 'loues' for 'lives', which M makes.

l. 2 from bot. after 'directions' M rightly inserts 'from the state, and found all accidents concurringe with the directions'. P omits, by mistake arising from the repetition of the word 'directions'. 'The state' = 'the statement or written information (plans, number of troops, &c.) supplied to the commanding officer for his guidance'. This I believe to be the meaning which is illustrated, though not exactly matched, by the use of the expression in modern regimental life. The only other interpretation that seems possible is that 'state' = 'staff'; cp. *l'état-major*. 'Government,'

'Government,' whether the English or the Dutch or that of Gravelines, makes no real sense.

122, l. 3. *Sinon* M : *Simon* P. The reference is, of course, to the story of the deceit of Sinon in Virgil, *Aeneid*, bk. ii.

l. 11. diversion=turning away; cp. 'diverting', p. 120, l. 3 from bot.

l. 14. which P : as M.

123, par. 2, l. 7. P prints 'Lieuetenant'.

124, l. 5 from bot. in M: at P. with P : by M.

125, l. 8. M inserts 'Count' before 'Hollock'.

l. 3 from bot. M inserts 'prouoked' before 'beyond', probably rightly.

126, par. 2, l. 4. M omits 'and art'.

l. 5. M reads 'sufficiencie', perhaps rightly, but unnoticed by Grosart.

l. 10. Grosart makes the extraordinary suggestion 'qu. advantage?' for 'disadvantage'. The sense obviously is that Sidney might have raised himself at Leicester's expense.

127, par. 2, l. 3. alayed M : allyed P. 'allayed' ='alloyed', cp. p. 161 last line.

par. 2, l. 8. to P : of M.

128, l. 13. this unenvious *Themistocles*] The reference here is to the story (told by Plutarch, *Vita Them.*, iii), that the fame won by Miltiades at Marathon caused such a change in the daily habits of Themistocles that his friends inquired the reason; to whom he replied that 'the trophy of Miltiades did not let him sleep'.

l. 9 from bot. M omits 'had'. Grosart erroneously refers the omission to the word 'resolved'.

129, par. 2, last line. M omits 'any'.

131, l. 2.

## Notes 255

131, l. 2. sensible natured = sensible of, or sensitive to, pain.

132, l. 1. the same P : that M.

l. 11. M inserts 'unexpected' before 'words', and 'in a distracted passion' before ' cries '.

133, ll. 3 foll. I follow P, which makes a good, though quaintly expressed sense. ' Unworthiness' is the author of the Florentine proverb (' Amicizia riconciliata piaga mal saldata,' as Grosart quotes). M reads ' buried with worthines, the author of it, or at least the practice, cryed down '; but ' with worthines' is an unmeaning tautology with 'worthily'. Grosart has an unintelligible reading 'practise it' and an unintelligible note 'P, ' practise' ".

par. 2, l. 5. M omits ' of'.

l. 6. stang P : stunge M. The phrase = ' the pangs with which his wounds stung him'.

l. 7. P has a comma after 'together'.

134, l. 12. M omits ' presently'.

l. 2 from bot. artificers P : artists M: artistes Grosart, who erroneously says that P has 'artifices'.

135, l. 5. M inserts 'utterly' before ' cast'.

136, l. 9. racke M : rake P.

l. 10. M inserts 'reason of' before ' sorrow' and transposes 'hardly' and 'being'.

l. 9 from bot. M and P agree in reading ' bent', which seems to mean ' tension', though I find no parallel to such a use of the substantive. ' Eternity so much affected' = 'the so great desire of eternity'.

137, l. 14. P misprints ' externall' for ' eternall'.

138, l. 8. or P : and M.

l. 10 from bot. and by that P : and by the and by the M.

l. 5 from bot. Contemplations P : Contemplation

plation (or rather, as M habitually writes words of this termination, 'contemplacōn') M.
    138, last line. between P : of M.
    139, l. 3. M omits 'of'.
       l. 8 from bot. his P : this M.
       l. 6 from bot. with P : in M.
    140, l. 6. this P : the M.
       l. 8. Scene P : line of M. The 'of' is perhaps correct.
       l. 8 from bot. as they honoured, &c.] The general sense of the sentence is clearly that it was likely enough that Sidney might have become Duke of the United Netherlands, as the following passage shows: but the sentence looks hardly correct, though M and P agree. As it stands, the construction must be, 'there was such a sympathy that they honoured that worth of Sir Philip, owing to which [worth or honour?] time and occasion would have been likely...'
    141, l. 2. become M : come P. The phrase 'in time to come' is unexceptionable in itself, but the words 'to become' are needed for the construction.
    par. 2, l. 2. can P : may M.
       l. 3 from bot. states of few, or many = Oligarchy or Democracy, the latter being called on the next page, l. 9, Popularitie.
       l. 2 from bot. M omits 'be', and has 'to' added only above the line, writing originally 'forsake the same'.
    last line. M omits 'having'.
    142, l. 2. M omits 'naturall'.
       l. 10. forced P : enforced againe M, unnoticed by Grosart.
       l. 11. Monarchs M : Monarchies P.
                              142, l. 16.

p. 142, l. 16. lest P: *whether* M, as if doubtful. [least]
  l. 17. competencie=competition, as Grosart says; cp. p. 160, l. 7.
  143, l. 5. mettals P. M has 'comodities' scratched out and 'mettalls' written over.
  par. 2, l. 1. or P: and M.
  l. 9 from bot. M inserts 'at' before 'first', not noticed by Grosart.
  l. 5 from bot. only is the P: is the only M, not noticed by Grosart.
  l. 2 from bot. interested P: intressed M, which Grosart reports as 'interested'.
  144, l. 4. then=than. Hitherto P has printed 'than', the last place being p. 138, l. 8, but henceforth it prints 'then'. Also at the heading of Chapters it changes from 'Chap.' to 'Cap.' The differences probably existed in the MS. from which P was printed.
  145, l. 5. M omits 'or good will', and 'own' in next line.
  par. 2, l. 2. homage P. M has 'happines' scratched out and 'homage' following.
  l. 3 from bot. According to modern habits of punctuation, we should omit the commas at 'birth' and 'time', and insert one after 'breeding'.
  146, l. 5. P misprints 'propriest' for 'properest'.
  l. 12. P has a comma after 'Governesse'.
  147, par. 2, l. 7. The metaphor 'steales where it cannot trade' is not too unexpected for Greville, otherwise one might be tempted to read 'tread', comparing P's misprint on p. 100, l, 1.
  par. 2, l. 10. stayed P: taxed M.
  148, l. 9. anything M: nothing P.
  148, l. 10.

148, l. 10. of Government, as well as P : as well of Gouernment as of M. Grosart has the facts wrong.
149, l. 1. Prince P : Princesse M.
l. 8. M omits 'the'.
l. 10. be forced either P : either be forced M. Grosart wrongly says that M omits 'either'.
l. 7 from bot. his P : the M.
l. 6 from bot. planted P : placed M.
l. 5 from bot. those P : theis M.
l. 3 from bot. M inserts 'to' before 'bound'.
150, l. 12. this kind of writing P : theis kind of writeings M.
l. 3 from bot. though P : that M.
151, l. 5. self- P : safe M.
l. 12. their P : the M.
l. 3 from bot. M omits 'to' before 'cure', having first written 'excuse' by mistake after 'then' and then scratched it out.
l. 2 from bot. Grosart inserts 'some' before 'reason', without comment and without authority of M or P.
152, l. 9. more P : other M.
l. 10. was P : is M.
l. 9 from bot. M omits 'and'.
153, l. 3. extremities P : extreames M.
l. 7. Metaphysicall P : Metaphoricall M, Grosart. Greville uses 'Metaphysicall' simply to mean 'philosophical'. Phormio was the philosopher who lectured Hannibal on the art of war, provoking the comment of Hannibal that he had seen many crazy old men but none so crazy as Phormio.
par. 2, ll. 1-3. Greville alludes to the lines of Horace, *Epistles* ii. 2. 187-189 .. Scit Genius, natale

natale comes, qui temperat astrum, | Naturae deus humanae, mortalis in unum | Quodque caput....

153, par. 2, l. 6. selfe P : spirittes M.

154, l. 2. M transposes 'men' and 'commonly'.

l. 4. utmost P : uttermost M.

l. 6 from bot. M omits 'or discourses'.

155, l. 2. limme=limb, a fairly common spelling in the sixteenth century. For the rarer converse cp. *Epistle Dedicatory* l. 3.

l. 3. Treatises M : Treatics P.

l. 10. deriuatives M : derivations P.

l. 16. these P : those M. The whole of this sentence is one of the most obscure. The general sense is that on reconsidering his poems Greville found that the political treatises had spread to such an unwieldy size that he left them as they stood without attempting further to lick them into shape (cp. p. 153, par. 2, l. 4). But the phrase 'of our old Pope, the sin', seems unintelligible. Was any particular sin ever called 'the sin' *par excellence*? Pride or Vanity (cp. the following lines) seems the only conceivable candidate. One cannot help suspecting that the text is corrupt; but as yet I can see no possible emendation.

l. 4 from bot. to P : in M.

156, l. 3. 'The Astronomers pit' refers to the well-known Greek story of Thales falling into a well.

par. 2, l. 3. P misprints 'Poets, metamorphosing'. M inserts 'of' after 'metamorphosing', and it makes the sense clearer.

l. 7 from bot. Grosart misprints 'even' for 'ever'.

l. 5 from bot. such P : such a M. Grosart omits 'such', as if following M.

157, l. 3.

157, l. 3. this P: that M.
l. 11. tumble upon their Soveraignes Circles = intrude upon the sacred prerogatives of Royalty; cp. p. 174, l. 7. This use of 'circle' is a favourite one with Greville; cp. p. 85, l. 2 from bot., p. 126, bottom.

par. 2, l. 4. *Laesa Majestas* P: Laesae Majestatis M.

158, line 3. P misprints 'time' for 'line'.
l. 8. these P: those M, perhaps rightly.
l. 12. *Prosopopeias* = Personifications. It does not clearly appear what Greville means. He was sent to Rochester to guard a figurative (i. e. fictitious) fleet, which was in danger of nothing except these personifications of (fictitious enemies imagined by?) invisible rancour (the Cecils and Raleigh, enemies of Essex?).
l. 13. M inserts 'it were' after 'as'.
l. 6 from bot. lead P: tend M.

159, l. 3. '*unreturning* steps' alludes to the fable of the fox and the lion in Horace, *Epistles* i. 1. 74:

Quia me vestigia terrent
Omnia te adversum spectantia, nulla retrorsum.

par. 2, l. 3. temporary *Neptunes*: the reference is chiefly to Sir Walter Raleigh, whom Essex regarded as his chief rival. The allusion in 'Creator of Admiralls' is to the Cecils, and to the elevation of Lord Howard of Effingham to the rank of Lord High Admiral, which, when he was subsequently made Earl of Nottingham, gave him precedence over Essex. The whole of this passage may be illuminated by reference to the Life of Essex by Sidney Lee in *D.N.B.*

159, par. 2, l. 6.

## Notes

159, par. 2, l. 6. his P: that M.
 l. 7 war=fight.
 l. 2 from bot. publique Actions P: accōns publicke M.
 160, l. 2. Martiall=marshal.
 l. 7. competency=competition: cp. p. 142, l. 17.
 l. 9. factious English P: English factions M.
 l. 10. M omits 'all'.  to M: in P.
 161, l. 1. M inserts 'the' before 'falling'.
 l. 8. M omits 'that', probably rightly, as no particular party seems to be meant.
 par. 2, l. 3. selling P: filling M. Grosart calls 'selling' a mis-reading, but it is clearly right.
 l. 6. Grosart misprints 'treating' for 'creating'.
 162, ll. 1 foll. If the text is correct, this extraordinary utterance must, apparently, mean, 'now after this humble and harmless desire of myself, a humble subject, to avoid the dangers of a career of action, which I have expressed in describing the errors of the Earl of Essex, a great subject, and his fall, which was brought about by the dark machinations of courtiers. . . .'
 l. 12. avow M: know P.
 l. 4 from bot. Legall M: Regall P. For the phrase 'Legall and Royall' cp. p. 191, l. 3 from bot.
 163, l. 4. P omits 'a'.
 l. 8. M omits 'with' and reads 'mutenies' (Grosart 'muteines').
 l. 11. M omits 'to show all to be infected about them'.
 l. 14. M omits 'with true obedience'.
 164, l. 5. Benefield] Sir Henry Bedingfield, Constable of the Tower.
          164, l. 7.

164, l. 7. M inserts ' a ' before ' free given '.
l. 10 from bot. perscribed P, Grosart. The reading of M is doubtful, the abbreviation for per- and pre-being the same : cp. ' precipitate ' on p. 165, l. 8.
l. 9 from bot. and P : in M, Grosart, wrongly.
165, l. 12. Princelike P : princely M.
166, l. 8. revives P : releiues M, written with some hesitation at the ' le '. ' revives' in P may be a reminiscence of p. 165, last line ; but is quite likely to be right.
l. 5 from bot. Noune adjective nature : cp. p. 107, l. 8 from bot.
l. 4 from bot. proceeded P : proceedes M, probably rightly ; cp. the rest of the paragraph.
167, l. 8. M omits ' of '.
l. 9 from bot. M inserts ' at home ' after ' faction '. It may be right, but I believe it is a mistaken repetition from the previous clause.
168, l. 2. Refers to the League of Henry VIII and Charles V in 1543.
l. 6. The ' Astronomicall, or rather biaced division of the world ' refers to ' the Bull of Pope Alexander VI, which divided between the Portuguese and Castillian monarchs the World about to be discovered, laying down an imaginary line to the west of the Azores as the boundary " ; A.D. 1493. —Helps, *Spanish Conquest of America*, iii. 67.
l. 12. M inserts ' the ' before ' persecucōn '.
l. 2 from bot. Brill, Bril, or Briel, in S. Holland, on a branch of the Maas, near its mouth.
170, l. 6. the P : of M.
l. 11. M inserts ' many wayes ' before ' distressed '.
l. 14. by P : in M.

170, l. 15.

# Notes

170, l. 15. the *Holland* P. : Holland's M.

l. 9 from bot. as I said once before)] p. 57, l. 7. The whole sentence means that Elizabeth thought a combination of France and Holland might be more dangerous than Spain had hitherto been. 'Our entised undertakings, or abandoned retraits' seems to refer to such expeditions as that of Sir John Norris in support of Don Antonio.

last line. averre P: avow M.

171, l. 5. M inserts 'especially buttressed with such stronge partyes abroad' after 'home' (Grosart misprints 'strange').

l. 7. yet P : yea M, Grosart, destroying the sense. M. has 'the' for 'they', as in several other places.

l. 8. P omits 'the' before 'Church', and in next line has a full stop after 'doe'.

l. 26. which P : that M.

l. 5 from bot. As noted before, the punctuation is puzzling to a modern reader: the construction is 'ordained to devour'. the other P : another M, Grosart; a mere slip in M.

last line. M inserts 'Hereupon' or perhaps 'Thereupon' before 'She', to the improvement of the sense.

172, par. 2, l. 1. Upon P : After M.

l. 5 from bot. *Cales* = Cadiz; cp. p. 92, l. 9. It is worth noticing that M here first wrote 'Callice' (i. e. Calais) and then scratched it out and substituted 'Cales'.

l. 4 from bot. and P : or M. Grosart says, 'P grossly misreads " and " '; but the two forms of expression are equally idiomatic and almost equally ungrammatical.

l. 2 from bot. to P : from M. The difference is

is less important than it might appear, as Drake after his attack on Cadiz captured the fortifications of Cape St. Vincent, and made Sagres Bay, just to the east, his base of operations for a time. The 'three forts' are probably those of Sagres, St. Vincent, and Valliera; and the 'carricke' a few lines further on is the *San Felipe*, the King of Spain's own East Indiaman, the greatest prize Drake ever took; cp. Corbett's *Drake*, vol. ii. pp. 94 and 107.

173, l. 6. journey P : voyage M.
l. 7. spoile P : spoiles M.
l. 11 from bot. presidents = precedents, as p. 69 l. 8 from bot.
l. 7 from bot. curiously P : cautiously M. Grosart says, ' P. grossly misreads " curiously " ' ; but it is very doubtful if P is wrong. At any rate, ' curiously ' is slightly the better word here. I think Greville probably wrote ' over ' and not ' ever '.
l. 4 from bot. M omits ' fraile '.

174. This page contains one long sentence, though P prints a full stop at 'motions', l. 12. The meaning after l. 7 may be given shortly thus: Elizabeth left the comparative prerogatives of Royalty and Parliament to sleep along with those aspiring spirits who had in previous times tried to upset the balance and had forced her ancestors to act with doubtful legality and policy towards Parliament, sometimes using the Nobles to master the people and sometimes the people to make the Nobles yield.

l. 11 from bot. Session : Wherein P: cessation: where M, Grosart. P has the better reading. The envy of the other members of the House of Commons is caused by one of their number being called up

# Notes

up to the Lords. It is no question of the 'recess', as Grosart appears to think in following M.

175, ll. 4–6. Greville here perhaps alludes to the incident in the affair of Henry VIII and Catharine of Aragon, when on Cranmer's advice Henry sent round to ask the opinions of all the European universities on the question whether his marriage with Catharine had been legal or not. Henry and the Emperor each obtained a verdict favourable to himself from the universities which he could control by threats or bribery. The fact that this 'Canvasse' actually affected the legitimacy of Queen Elizabeth's birth need not have been present to Greville's mind as an objection to such an allusion. On the other hand he may be merely drawing a metaphor from the intrigues of university politics.

par. 2, l. 8. M omits 'or besides'.

l. 12. P misprints 'Petitionet'.

176, l. 1. 'a quintessence,' &c. is not the object of 'foresaw', but in opposition to 'wisdome of Government': the sentence is taken up again in l. 4, where the full stop is, according to modern punctuation, ungrammatical.

l. 5 from bot. strengths P : strength M ; cp. p. 5, l. 4.

last line. 'Anti-Rome.' As often, Greville combines two points in one, however heterogeneous. He wishes to use the illustration of Remus leaping over the newly built wall of Rome, and the word Rome at once suggests its ecclesiastical sense, in which it is the opposite of the structure which Elizabeth was trying to build up.

177, l. 6. P inserts 'a' before 'foreseeing', perhaps from a loosely written 'e' at the end of 'seeme' in the original MS.

177, l. 6 from bot. vainly M : vanity P.
l. 2 from bot. threatned M : threaten P.
a P : the M. The meaning is that these 'confusions' might seem ignorant passions and such as threatened nothing less than a loss of the liberties of the people, which they had inherited just as much as she had inherited her crown.

178, l. 3. M omits 'and her Ancestors'.
l. 6. M inserts 'to raigne' before 'over'.
l. 10. or P : and M.
l. 10 from bot. by P : with M.
l. 6 from bot. P places a comma before, and none after, 'there.'
l. 5 from bot. M inserts 'discoūed' (apparently for 'discovered', as Grosart prints) before 'discredited'.
last line. M omits 'all'.

179, l. 4. M inserts 'all' before 'her'.
l. 5. ever P : never M.
l. 9 from bot. M omits 'Predecessor' : Grosart does not notice the omission.
l. 8 from bot. miscarriage P : carriage M, the simpler reading, and perhaps right. At any rate 'miscarriage' must mean 'evil behaviour', not 'failure'.
l. 5 from bot. runne P : rome M.
l. 2 from bot. rest P : restes M. Both the singular and plural are favourite words with Greville.

180, l. 2. violence P : violences M.
l. 3. defects P : deserts M.
l. 7. their P : other M, Grosart, without sense.
l. 8. M inserts 'being' before 'excepted'.
l. 14. M inserts 'the' before 'earth'. It is not

not easy to decide between the two, very different, meanings: but on the whole I prefer P's reading.

180, l. 18. to P: of M, Grosart, without sense. The construction is 'be forced to traffic for a younger brother's, not an heir's, place.' The allusion is, of course, to the story of Esau: but in the subsequent clause Greville throws in a new allusion, the 'wide gates' of the Roman Church being compared, of course, to the 'wide gate, which leadeth to destruction'. In the following sentence the illustration again shifts its ground, and is taken from the distinction between sons and servants, especially prominent in St. Paul's teaching.

l. 19. an heires P: a coheires M.

l. 7 from bot. he=Henry IV of France, the general reflections arising out of his apostasy here gliding back into his particular case.

181, l. 7 from bot. holy M: hollow P. 'Hollow' seems inappropriate here.

l. 4 from bot. the striving *Alexanders* of time present] Cp. p. 211, l. 16.

l. 3 from bot. Grosart puts a comma at 'passing' without authority, and destroying the sense. 'passing finely' = 'very finely'. Cp. p. 186, par. 2, l. 3.

182, l. 12. Where P: Whence M.

l. 3 from bot. M has 'ministers of justice' written and scratched out before 'distributers'.

183, l. 2. superstitious P: suspicious M. In another writer one would accept M's reading without question, but Greville uses 'superstitious' often and is quite capable of giving it such a meaning as 'unworthy, like false religion, of credit'.

par. 2, l. 7. the P: their M.

183, last line.

183, last line. 'by their places' apparently = 'in due order, distinctly'.

184, l. 1. Nature M: Natures P.

l. 2. reall M: deep P. 'deep' is perhaps tempting as the *lectio exquisitior*, but 'reall businesse' is Greville's style.

l. 9 from bot. their P: the M.

l. 5 from bot. P misprints 'Polarke'.

185, l. 2. a P: any M.

l. 3. M inserts 'and' before 'againe'.

l. 6. M omits 'entire to her selfe'.

par. 2, l. 7. M omits 'power and'.

l. 8. her P: a M.

l. 11. eyes P: eye M.

l. 8 from bot. The reference is to the marriage of Burghley's granddaughter Lady Lucy Cecil, daughter of Thomas, Earl of Exeter, with William, fourth Marquis of Winchester, great-grandson of Burghley's predecessor as Lord Treasurer, William Paulet, first Marquis of Winchester. Greville's phraseology is curious, as Paulet had long been dead when this marriage took place.

l. 4 from bot. Copyholds P: Copyholders M.

l. 3 from bot. M omits 'to take hold'.

last line. Grosart has an erroneous note that M omits 'what soever'.

186, l. 3. M omits 'and'.

l. 13. will P: would M.

l. 15. M inserts 'private' before 'Exchequer'.

l. 17. inned = gathered in, a fairly common use till the eighteenth century.

par. 2, l. 3. graces P: grauntes M, probably rightly.

l. 2 from bot. circuit P: circles M. 'circles' is a favourite word with Greville, especially
in

in connexion with monarchy: but 'circuit' may be right here.
187, l. 4. or P: and M.
par. 2, l. 1. her P: the M.
l. 6. her M: their P.    Royalties P: Regallities M.
l. 3 from bot. reverend M: reverent P.
last line. out of M: in P.
188, l. 1. upon P: against M.
l. 14. M inserts 'any' before 'present', and writes 'extremity'.
par. 2, l. 3. M inserts 'of' before 'honour', and Grosart follows.
l. 4. State P: estate M.
189, l. 4. M inserts 'chiefe' after 'other'.
l. 6. punishments P: punishment M.
par. 3, l. 3. another P: the other M.
l. 4. her P: the M.
l. 5. Liveries P: libertyes M, Grosart.
l. 6 from bot.   M has the modern spelling 'Yeomanry', unnoticed by Grosart.
l. 5 from bot.   Nobles P: Noblesse M.
190, l. 3. champion countrey = unenclosed, common land (cp. *N.E.D.*), and is opposed to the 'fences' of the next clause, both being, of course, metaphorical.
l. 10. those P: theis M (i.e. these).   Grosart reads 'them', without meaning.
191, l. 1. M inserts 'his' after 'Pythagoras', making the construction clear at first sight: of course 'Pythagoras' is in the possessive case, though P, as usual, does not mark it. The allusion is to one of the 'golden sayings' of Pythagoras, that the paths of Virtue and of Vice resemble the letter Ч (the old form of ϒ or Y); that of Virtue being

being the arduous one straight up, that of Vice the one leading more gently off to the left. This, with other picturesque traditions of Pythagoras, is banished from our modern books of reference, but may be found in older works; or see Conington on Persius iii. 56. Greville applies the saying to the different width of the right and left hand strokes of the Y with an obvious reminiscence of the Christian contrast of the broad and the narrow ways.

191, par. 2, l. 9. indennize P : endemnize M, Grosart. Cotgrave has 'indemnize'='indemnify', which makes no sense here; whereas 'indenize' here has the meaning 'kidnap', 'spirit away,' or 'translate' (cp. *N.E.D.*). The allusion in the following words is to the proverbial quibble about the Delia, a trireme used for sacred embassies, traditionally dating from the time of Theseus, and constantly patched, so that, according to Plutarch, it was used as a proverb for things that were always and yet never the same. Greville uses the same image in his *Caelica* (Sonnet lxxxiv):

> The ship of Greece, the streame, and she be not the same
> They were, although ship, streame, and she still bear their antique name.
> The wood which was, is worne; the waves are run away,
> Yet still a ship, and still a streame, still running to a sea.
> She lov'd, and still she loves, but doth not still love me;
> To all except my selfe yet is, as she was wont to be.

191, l. 4

# Notes

191, l. 4 from bot. or P: and M.
l. 2 from bot. state P: stiles M, Grosart.
192, l. 4. averse M: adverse P. Grosart by mistake reads 'adverse' in his text; hence his note 'P, "adverse,"' is unintelligible. The same remark applies to par. 2, l. 3, below, where M reads 'power'.
l. 6. Taxe P: taxes M.
l. 8. or P: and M.
l. 10. M omits 'or wish her to be'.
par. 2, l. 3. M omits 'the'.
l. 8. M omits 'in', and so improves the grammar: but the negligence is quite like Greville.
l. 7 from bot. P prints 'nature; Education', making 'Education and Practice' the 'mixtures of nature' referred to. Though sense could be made of this, I have no doubt Greville meant the other; he would not fail to include Elizabeth's 'Nature' as one of the elements of her success; indeed he has just referred to it in the words 'long and happy descent', &c.
193, l. 9. M omits 'the'.
l. 15. I have inserted semicolons at 'blotting' and 'depressing' to save the sense. Another way would be to place commas at those words, and remove them after 'writing', 'raising,' and 'reall'.
l. 8 from bot. want P: lacke M.
l. 4 from bot. the raising of P: to raise M.
l. 3 from bot. Monarch P: Monarchs M. Perhaps we should read 'Monarchy'.
194, l. 4. M inserts 'all' before 'Sabbaths'.
l. 7. she M: they P.
l. 8. M inserts 'and' before 'transforme', perhaps rightly.

194, l. 10.

194, l. 10. fortune P : forme M, perhaps rightly.
l. 5 from bot. irregularly M : irregularitie P.
l. 4 from bot. climbe P : claime M, Grosart.
195, l. 1. M writes 'wanting' first; then scratches out 'ing' and writes 'on', and finally scratches all out and writes 'wanton'.
l. 7. any P : in a M.
l. 14. M inserts 'like' before 'a'.
l. 15. sweate M : sweet P.
l. 16. M inserts 'the' before 'humble', unnoticed by Grosart.
l. 7 from bot. 'Merchant' is here an adjective.
last line. of P : in M.
196, l. 3. the benefit of P : benefite M.
l. 9. M omits 'and'.
l. 11. wherein they have and P : under which they liue and doe M.
par. 2, l. 3. slavish P : lauish M. Grosart calls 'slavish' a gross misprint : but either word is quite possible here.
l. 5 from bot. this P : that M.
l. 4 from bot. I follow Grosart in printing 'Time-presents' as one word, though P prints 'time presents', as the ambiguity of the latter is confusing, though the sense is necessarily clear on reflection.
197, l. 4. M omits 'side'.
par. 2, l. 4. P prints commas before and after 'all'.
l. 5. M reads 'which' by mistake for 'with'.
l. 9. M inserts 'the' before 'most'.
l. 11. Government P : governments M.
l. 6 from bot. equally P : equall M.
198, l. 3. M omits 'in'.
198, l. 12.

198, l. 12. Coast P : coasts M.
l. 14. M spells ' Ordinance ' here and elsewhere.
199, l. 7. M omits ' of '.
par. 2, l. 5. men, M : new P.
l. 7 from bot. *Groniland* P : Groenland M · = Greenland.
200, ll. 2 foll. This passage is corrupt. M has a considerable number of words which are not in P, but does not clear up the difficulty. M reads : ' whose experience she knew taught them how to husband and guide her *Muscovy* Company in generall Provisions, not as partner with her Merchants, but to governe instrumentall servantes and services with skill, the Master shipwrights not only in building, but restraining the Ship-keepers riot, or expence in harbour,' &c. The general sense is that Elizabeth chose distinguished naval men for her Admiralty Office, men who could properly supervise the proceedings of shipwrights, skippers, &c.
l. 9. martiall P : marshall M. Both intend the same verb. Cp. p. 160, l. 2 where Martiall = marshal, the substantive.
par. 2, l. 3. ' moulds ' = in modern phrase ' types ' of vessels.
l. 9. munition P : munitions M.
l. 10. of P . for M.
201, l. 2. tackling P · tackle M.
l. 3. Gunners P : Gunner M.   with P : and M.
l. 13. M inserts ' I ' before ' my '.
l. 15. M inserts ' the imployments of ' before ' my '.
l. 16. After ' it ' M has the following sentence

tence: 'Besides like a provident lady who knew Place, for the ease of Crownes, must serve both to reward meritt and to encourage it with other like motiues mentioned before [1], in the gouernment of the Exchequer, she kept her Cinque Portes seuered from the greatnes of the Admiralty, though she knew the principal vse and end in keeping of them devided were taken away by tyme and other changes through her sister's neglect and our former vnfortunate losses in Fraunce.'

201, par. 2, l. 1. M omits 'great'.
l. 2. high P : greate M.
l. 3. Patents P : lres. Patt[es] M.
last line. M omits 'their'.
202, par. 2, l. 4. insensible P : sencible M.
l. 3 from bot. with P : by M.
203, l. 4. part P : state M.
l. 7. M inserts 'and' before 'assisted'.
par. 3, l. 1. succession P : successe M.
l. 4. M omits 'first'.
l. 3 from bot. Inconsistency in punctuation is well illustrated by this paragraph in P, in which, though there are three co-ordinate sentences and a change of subject, there is no stronger stop than a comma.

204, l. 2. studied P : laboured M. In view of 'studied' in l. 6, it seems likely enough that Greville's first MS. had 'studied', and that he altered it to 'laboured' in a later draft. The paragraph as a whole does not run as we should expect, whether we leave the punctuation alone, or place a semicolon after 'Statutes', or place semicolons after both 'Statutes' and 'Princes'.

[1] Cp. p. 186.

204, par. 2, l. 3.

204, par. 2, l. 3. M omits 'intire'.
l. 7. P omits 'a'.
l. 7 from bot. wind-blown=full of wind like a bladder or cloud, hollow and puffed up. Cp. p. 109, l. 8; p. 211, l. 3.
l. 2 from bot. waved: cp. p. 174, l. 4 from bot.
205, par. 2, l. 4. neither P: not M.
207, l. 6. the Groyne = Coruña.
l. 10. *Peniche* (spelled Penicke in P), on the W. coast of Portugal.
l. 12. gates of the High Towne P: gates, took East Cales M, Grosart. This is a curious variant. There is no question of Cadiz here. It seems possible that the original MS. had some reference to *Cascaes*, at the mouth of the Tagus, where Drake lay cooperating with the land force which attacked Lisbon.
par. 2, l. 4. Netherlands P: Netherlanders M.
208, par. 2, l. 1. the meane P: this meane M.
l. 6. Leaguers M: Leagues P. 'Leaguers' or 'League' would be equally possible expressions, but hardly 'Leagues', in reference to the well-known 'League', referred to again below, l. 6 from bot.
209, l. 9. P omits 'and'.
par. 2, l. 7. M inserts 'and' before 'even', spoiling the construction.
210, l. 2. fearfull wings of this growing Monarch P: growing wings of his fearfull monarchie M. With P's reading cp. 'growing Monarchs' below, par. 2, l. 4, p. 211, l. 8.
l. 3. This must apparently mean 'made him borrow a great deal of money', but the phrase would more naturally be used of a prosperous investor.

T 2   210, par. 2, l. 9.

210, par. 2, l. 9. P misprints 'Granoda'.
l. 18. wisdome so P: wisdomes too M.
211, l. 2. M inserts 'Spanish' before 'Holofernes'.
l. 7. M omits 'and', and in l. 9 'the'.
l. 11. usuall M: usefull P. 'Usefull' could only be satirical, and does not seem to be in Greville's style. Leiger Embassadors = ledger-ambassadors, i.e. resident ambassadors as opposed to special envoys. The phrase is common in the sixteenth and seventeenth centuries.
l. 14. M omits 'so', probably rightly. M also reads 'those' for 'such' in l. 15, and brackets from 'like' to 'members' as a parenthesis. For the previous comparison of the Roman Church to Bucephalus cp. p. 181 near the bottom.
l. 4 from bot. unnaturall M: naturall P, by mistake.
l. 2 from bot. her P: their M, Grosart, wrongly.
last line. beame = beam of a balance, as the succeeding words show.
212, l. 5. Meeres = boundaries. Grosart compares Bacon's Essays, no. 56 [near the beginning: 'The mislaier of a Meere Stone is to blame'].
l. 6. the P: that M. procession M: precession P. The phrase 'to go procession' used to be common and is still in use locally for beating the bounds of a parish: and in view of the word 'meeres' it seems probable that Greville is using 'procession' in this sense here.
par. 2. l. 7. high P: huge M.
last line. Should not 'her' be 'him'? Though the other sovereigns might be said to be about Elizabeth as well as about Philip, the logic of

of the sentence makes it more natural to speak of them as about Philip.

212, l. 5 from bot. The reference is to the story of Aphrodite protecting Aeneas, not with a shield, but with her robe, and being herself wounded by Diomede : *Iliad*, v. 311 foll. Greville implies that if Elizabeth had fought Spain from under some 'Goddess' shield', the 'Goddess' might have met with the treatment received by Aphrodite ; but what does the 'goddess' of the metaphor represent? Apparently nothing more than Elizabeth's good fortune, or any supernatural assistance : but then the parenthetical semi-humorous addition seems to have no substantial meaning.

l. 3 from bot. This 'gallant Factor (agent) of her Merchants' was either William Harborne (cp. note to p. 24, l. 15) or his successor Edward Barton, who was agent 1588–1597. I have not been able to trace the incident to which Greville refers.

213, l. 3. yet, and upon P: yea upon M.

l. 4. zecchins P. chickeens M. Cp. 'Duckets' on p. 209, l. 6.

par. 2, l. 9. the heathen P : that heathen M.

l. 3 from bot. M omits 'both' and 'the' before 'living'.

215, l. 3. I have added a comma after 'justly'. M writes 'and justly' in brackets.

par. 2, l. 6. memories P: memory M. 'their memories' = the memories of Greville's *Antony and Cleopatra*.

par. 3, l. 2. M omits 'rather'.

l. 4 from bot. M inserts 'that' before 'no'.

l. 2 from bot. of asking P : to aske M.

216, l. 7. resolutions P : revolutions M, probably rightly, though Greville might use 'resolutions'

tions' to mean 'changes'. Note, however, 'resolution' below, l. 17.

216, l. 17. in P : on M.

par. 2, l. 1. curiously M : seriously P. The general sense, and the evidently contrasted use of 'seriously' in l. 3 from bot. shows that M is right here. 'Curiously' means 'out of curiosity'.

l. 3 from bot. demurr'd = dwelt upon : a common use in sixteenth and seventeenth centuries.

l. 2 from bot. in P : of M. Grosart by misprint interchanges, at the end of two successive lines, 'of' before 'his', with 'to' after 'superstition'.

217, l. 17. 'revive my self in her memory' of course means 'revive myself in remembering her'.

218, l. 10 from bot. my P : any M, Grosart, clearly wrongly.

219, l. 7. M inserts 'to be' after 'selfe'.

220, l. 12. M omits 'to' before 'put', probably rightly.

221, l. 4. exemplifie P : amplifie M, Grosart.

l. 5. Order P : orders M, Grosart.

l. 9. melancholike P : melancholy M. M inserts 'up' after 'stir'.

l. 7 from bot. M inserts 'of life' after 'practice'.

222, l. 1. errours P : errour M.

l. 6. talent. I do not know whether Greville is using 'talent', by false analogy from *ingenium*, in the sense of 'disposition', or whether we ought to emend 'intent'.

l. 7. M inserts 'the' before 'Poets'.

l. 8. P omits 'and' before 'all'.

l. 15. I have removed a comma after 'Sexe' to make the clause readily intelligible.

222, l. 11

222, l. 11 from bot. Unless 'Euripides' and 'Sophocles' have been transposed by clerical error, Greville must have been speaking of those dramatists only at second hand, and without remembering the traditional account of them. It is Euripides, of course, who has been, however inaccurately, regarded as a misogynist.

l. 4 from bot. M omits 'the', wrongly.

223, par. 2, l. 1. P omits 'though'. The reference is evidently to drawings with which Sidney embellished the margins of his *Arcadia*, which, as we all know, was widely circulated in MS.

l. 6. M inserts 'freely' before 'leave'.

l. 6 from bot. P inserts 'not' before 'too'.

224, l. 8. The black ox treading on a person's foot is given as a proverb for adversity first by J. Heywood (1562); Lyly in *Euphues* uses it along with the crow's foot about the eyes, cp. Nares' *Glossary*, or *N.E.D.* I do not know if the proverb is of English origin or not.

l. 15. thus M: this P.

l. 17. those P: theis M.

225, l. 8. large P: longe M.

l. 15. M omits 'the' before 'capacity'.

l. 7 from bot. I have removed a comma after 'worke', to get rid of an ambiguity of construction.

# BIBLIOLIFE

## Old Books Deserve a New Life
www.bibliolife.com

Did you know that you can get most of our titles in our trademark **EasyScript**™ print format? **EasyScript**™ provides readers with a larger than average typeface, for a reading experience that's easier on the eyes.

Did you know that we have an ever-growing collection of books in many languages?

Order online:
www.bibliolife.com/store

Or to exclusively browse our **EasyScript**™ collection:
www.bibliogrande.com

At BiblioLife, we aim to make knowledge more accessible by making thousands of titles available to you – quickly and affordably.

Contact us:
BiblioLife
PO Box 21206
Charleston, SC 29413

Printed in Great Britain
by Amazon.co.uk, Ltd.,
Marston Gate.